SALVAGE OF WATER DAMAGED BOOKS, DOCUMENTS, MICROGRAPHIC AND MAGNETIC MEDIA

A Case History - Dalhousie Univ. Law Library
Aug.1985

A Case History - Roanoke Virginia Flood
Nov.1985

First Edition
April 1986

ERIC G. LUNDQUIST, Owner/Founder

DOCUMENT REPROCESSORS
OF SAN FRANCISCO

41 Sutter St., Suite 1120
San Francisco, CA 94104

Tel: 415-362-1290 in CA

US Tollfree: 1-800-4 DRYING

Canada Tollfree: 1-800-5 DRYING

Document Reprocessors Publications April 1986

Library of Congress Cataloging in Publication Data

Lundquist, Eric G.;
*"Salvage of Water Damaged Books, Documents, Micrographic and
Magnetic Media"*
(a case history - Dalhousie Univ. Law Library Fire 1985
(a case history -- Roanoke Virginia Flood 1985)

(Document Reprocessors Publications)
1.   Books-Conservation and Restoration
2.   Manuscripts-Conservation and Restoration
3.   Business Documents-Conservation and Restoration
4.   Micrographics-Conservation and Restoration
5.   Magnetic Media-Conservation and Restoration

Illustrations by:
     Robert Ritchie
     Eric G. Lundquist
     Norman Fisher
     James D. Davies
     Ronald Kompera

Photography by Carlos

ISBN: 0-9616850-0-X

PREFACE

Dalhousie University Law Library Fire / Roanoke VA. Flood

The intention of this publication is to help prepare librarians, archivists, records managers, and others for the unlikely major disaster. The book discusses from first hand experience two major disasters, a fire at Dalhousie University, Halifax, Nova Scotia, and a flood in Roanoke, Virginia.

The Dalhousie University Law Library case history concerns a major fire which occurred in August 1985. Involved in the fire was the Law Library's entire collection of over 170,000 volumes. Close to 80,000 volumes were destroyed by the fire. Approximately 20,000 volumes were water and smoke damaged and in addition 70,000 volumes were only slightly wet, but had significant smoke damage. Also, all volumes were in random order as a result of uncontrollable pressures arising during the removal process. The book discusses details of how over 90,000 salvagable volumes (2 1/2 shelf miles) were dried and cleaned, and how, through [first time] use of computers, they were put back into shelf order by call number in 28 working days.

In November 1985 the Roanoke, Virginia area was deluged as a result of a 100 year storm. Water up to 14 feet deep flooded over 100 square miles of business and residential areas. The water damage to books and documents was more extensive than the Dalhousie fire. The method of salvage was markedly different as were the attitudes of the individuals, businesses and colleges involved. The differences were due to the nature of the disaster. The Roanoke case history was one of an area wide disaster; the Dalhousie Law Library fire was an isolated disaster. The differences in approach and solutions to the problems encountered in the area wide disaster at Roanoke are discussed in this book.

The reader should also note that there are two excellent books concerning salvage of library and record center materials and disaster planning. These are respectively: *Procedures for Salvage of Water-Damaged Library Materials* written in 1979 by Mr. Peter Waters, Head of the Conservation Department at the Library of Congress, Washington, DC, USA and *An Ounce of Prevention - A Handbook on Disaster Contingency Planning for Archives, Libraries, and Record Centers* published in 1985 by Mr. John Barton, Head Conservator, Archives of

iii

Ontario, Toronto, Ontario, Canada, and Ms. Johanna Wellheiser, Conservator, Metropolitan Toronto Library Board.

Salvage of Water Damaged Books, Documents, Micrographic and Magnetic Media, is based upon first hand experiences in salvaging major losses of library materials and business documents and fills the gap between Waters and the Barton/Wellheiser books with practical experience. It is hoped that it will become a desirable addition to the librarians' reference material for the handling of water and smoke damage problems.

Furthermore, this book discusses in depth the new and unique methods of salvage, including handling, cold storage alternatives, fumigation, mobile vacuum-freeze drying equipment, and computer useage for reassembling large collections of material, which have not previously been applied to solving such large scale problems. The experiences described demonstrate that 21st Century technology is commercially available at reasonable costs which will now enable large amounts of materials to be salvaged with almost 100% success.

ALL THAT MANKIND HAS DONE, THOUGHT, GAINED, OR BEEN:
IT IS LYING AS MAGIC PRESERVATION IN THE PAGES OF BOOKS.
THEY ARE THE CHOSEN POSSESSION OF MAN....CARLYLE.

Acknowledgments:

The author wishes to express his sincere appreciation for the invaluable assistance and encouragement afforded him during the preparation of this manuscript by the following persons. Without their assistance, this book would not have been possible.

Dalhousie University: Halifax, Nova Scotia	Dr. Andrew MacKay Dr. Bill Birdsall Dr. Fred Matthews Mr. Christian Wiktor Dr. Norman Horrocks Mr. Leslie Foster
ARMA International Standards Committee Prairie Village, Kansas	Mr. Robert Austin, CRM
The Atlantic Companies Roanoke, Virginia	Mr. Gerard Ferguson Mr. Jack Mahana
General Electric Credit Union Roanoke, Virginia	Mr. Charles Perkins Ms. Pamela Basham
Laramie County Clerk Cheyenne, Wyoming	Mrs. Janet Whitehead, CRM
Library of Congress Washington, D. C.	Mr. Peter Waters Dr. Robert McCombs
University of Calif. Berkeley, California	Mrs. Sally Buchanan Mr. John Morris
University of Texas Humanities Research Center Austin, Texas	Mr. Donald Etherington
Archives of Ontario Toronto, Ontario	Mr. John Barton
Metropolitan Toronto Library Board Toronto, Ontario	Ms. Johanna Wellheiser

TABLE OF CONTENTS

TABLE OF ILLUSTRATIONS

DALHOUSIE UNIVERSITY LAW LIBRARY
Halifax, Nova Scotia August 1985

Figure 1. Weldon Law Building before the fire - five floors

Figure 2. Weldon Law Building 3 weeks after the fire.
Note: Top floor is missing. The building is now four floors.

DALHOUSIE LAW LIBRARY

Fire Aug. 16, 1985   Halifax, Nova Scotia

Fact Sheet

Destroyed (Majority of Fifth Floor)	70000	volumes
Damaged (Entire Fourth Floor)	90000	volumes
Salvaged for Immediate Reshelving	89000	volumes
Unsalvagable	1000	volumes
Percentage Successfully Salvaged	98.8	percent
Contract Award Date		Aug. 24, 1985
Contract Completion Date		Sept.30, 1985
Duration of Contract		28 Workdays
Labor Expended		9000 manhrs
Workforce - Locally Hired		to 50 per day
Supervision - Document Reprocessors		5 supervisors

Scope of Work Performed:

Cleaning:	Edges and Covers	90000	volumes
Drying:	Air Dried	70000	volumes
	Drying Chamber	20000	volumes
Odor Control:	Removal of Smoke Odor	90000	volumes
Presorting:	Journals	30000	volumes
	LC Catagory	60000	volumes
Computer Entry:	LC Catagory	60000	volumes
Shelf Lists:	Journal	1500	boxes
	LC Catagory	2400	shelves

Note: This project was started at four different work sites.   Later consolidated to the 10,000 sq.ft. Studley Gym on Dalhousie Campus.

CHAPTER 1   DALHOUSIE UNIVERSITY DISASTER

The Fire and Initial Reactions

Disasters test the wills and patience of us all, not only to add to our normal duties, but to create confounding situations which place us in positions of having to make quick decisions, the results of which will determine the eventual level of success of the project.

Dr. Fred Matthews, retired Professor of Library Service and Disaster Team Coordinator at Dalhousie University, Halifax, Nova Scotia, Canada said:

> *"If you haven't done your homework prior to the disaster there is no time to do it once disaster strikes. It is fine to have Waters[1] and Barton/Wellheisers[2] books on the shelf, but the day of the disaster is too late to read them."*

The Barton/Wellheiser book-- *An Ounce of Prevention A Handbook on Disaster Contingency Planning for Archives, Libraries and Record Centres*, describes and defines those items which should be included in a plan when disaster strikes.

In the case of the Dalhousie Law Library, (fig 1,2) which contained the most complete collection on Maritime Law in Canada, a freak lightning storm struck the Halifax area in the early morning hours of Friday Aug. 16, 1985. The Law Library cleaning crew arrived on the scene at 7:00 AM, three hours after the storm and smelled smoke on the fifth (top) floor. (fig.3) Before they were even able to alert the local fire department, the entire fifth floor had become engulfed in a raging inferno consuming almost all of the collection of approximately 80,000 volumes. 90,000 additional volumes mainly from the fourth floor below, plus the shelf list would later be salvaged in an unprecedented effort taking a crew of 55 persons 28 working days and requiring over 9,000 manhours.

Figure 3. Dalhousie University Law Library Fire Aug. 16, 1985

Among the group who had gathered to observe the actions of the fire fighters were several extremely concerned individuals who heard the news while preparing for the day's work. There was little doubt in any of their minds while observing the blaze that they were faced with a task of major magnitude. At the impromptu meeting Dr. Andrew MacKay (University President), Innis Christie (Dean of the Law School), Dr. Louis Vagianos (former University Librarian), Dr. William Birdsall (University Librarian), Christian Wiktor (Law Librarian), and Dr. Fred Matthews, formed the nucleus of the Disaster Recovery Team to coordinate this major project, possibly the largest fire salvage effort ever attempted in North America.

Although the fire was under control by 10:00 AM, it would be some time before anyone from the University could safely enter the building to assess the extent of the damage incurred to the Law Library collection. It was apparent from the outside, however, that the damage to the books on the fifth floor would be extensive. (fig.4) Concerns about water damage to the books on the fourth floor were expressed to fire department officials. They responded by making every effort to minimize such damage. Calls were pouring in from University faculty, library employees, students, and concerned citizens volunteering to help with the clean up operations as they heard early morning broadcasts. Meanwhile, the Disaster Recovery Team set about doing what necessary tasks they could think of while the building was cooling off enough for them to enter. Details will be discussed in the next chapter.

Figure 4. Aerial view of fire damage, Dalhousie Law Library

Fire restoration specialist Jim Nichols of Digby, Nova Scotia recommended the services of Document Reprocessors, having learned about their work at a conference a few months earlier. The California firm was equipped to bring large capacity mobile drying equipment to the scene from their East Coast branch, and within hours the salvage effort was under way. It was important to get to the scene promptly to insure the successful salvage of as much of the collections as possible for this prestigious library.

The techniques used in meeting the emergency have written a new chapter in the history of library disaster recovery. There were many initial reactions to this disaster which would make library history. The most important reaction, whether there was a workable library disaster plan or not, was that quick, accurate decisions had to be made if anything was to be salvaged from the once prestigious library.

It was a time for action and courage.

CHAPTER 2

The Disaster Recovery Team

Who would have believed that a lightning strike could start a fire that might destroy the top floor of the library? Like many another library, disaster plans were less than complete, and an "ad hoc" emergency Disaster Recovery Team was hurriedly organized at the height of the fire. The decision makers for the library and the University were on the Team and remained actively involved in the restoration effort from start to finish. They knew what needed to be done, and in conjunction with the staff and volunteers who labored to remove damaged materials, did a capable job of managing the disaster, particularly in the early period following the fire.

In times of emergency, it is a credit to our ingenuity that we manage to pull together to make up for lost time. The disadvantage is that hastily laid plans often thrive on compromise and concession which result in either higher costs or less yield. Fortunately in the case of Dalhousie University there was little if any compromise to be made as the prime decision makers (those who were all on the Disaster Recovery Team) became and remained actively involved in the operation from start to finish and they knew what to do. The efficency of this operation is a further credit to the volunteers who initially removed the materials from the damaged library.

Several actions were instituted even before Fire Department officials allowed members of the Team to enter the building and survey the extent of damages. The Team would require boxes, manpower, trucks, and supervision to remove the books.

They knew from reading Waters book[3], **"To leave such materials more than 48 hours in temperatures above 70oF and humidity above 70 percent will almost certainly result in heavy mold growth..."** that once the wet books were removed from the library, they must be frozen as quickly as possible to arrest any bacterial growth until drying equipment could be brought on line and operating. This meant identifying freezer space.

Also, since all books had been exposed to excessive heat and humidity, those books not requiring freezing would still require some form of air drying. Hence, enough floor space would have to be obtained to spread out as many as 100,000 books (the original estimate) for air drying.

Local cardboard box companies agreed to supply whatever they could from their existing inventories, since there was not enough time to produce new boxes. This resulted in boxes of varying shapes and sizes, yet unfortunately only enough to contain half of the books. The lack of sufficient boxes ultimately added to the difficulties in the removal and relocation of materials from the damaged library.

Trucks were available from the University and space was set aside at a local cold storage company. A call for volunteers was put out over the local radio and television stations and those responding were directed to the Main Library for coordination into work teams.

Floor space was tentatively arranged for in a University residence hall study area; at the University's old main gymnasium (which was full of exercise equipment in use by the Physical Education Department); in a large hall in a church located adjacent to the campus; and finally at a dance studio beneath the gymnasium.

Things were taking shape even before the actual damages had been assessed.

CHAPTER 3

Survey of The Damage

At 1:00 PM the fire chief conducted the Diaster Recovery Team on a tour of the building. It was clear that there had been extensive water and smoke damage to all floors of the building. The elevators and electricity were out of service, and the trip up the stairs was like one through a tropical rain forest during the height of a storm, dark, humid, hot, with water pouring everywhere. Inspection of the fifth floor confirmed their worst fears. Most of the fifth floor law library was a smoldering mass of rubble. (fig.5) Those books remaining were badly fire damaged. (fig.6)

The fourth floor library stacks were a different matter. The 90,000 volumes contained there were clearly damaged by water and smoke, but there did appear to be hope for salvage of almost all of this, the most valuable and irreplaceable portion of the librarys' collection. In addition, the rare book collection was spared destruction as it was shelved in a locked room on the fourth floor.

Figure 5. Damage to the library on the fifth floor.

7

Credit is given to the Fire Department for protecting books not involved in the fire from excessive water damage by covering the shelves with tarpaulins until the books could be removed.

One of the things sought out during this early inspection tour was the library card catalogue. Unfortunately the author-title, and subject catalogues were destroyed on the fifth floor, but the shelf list was intact, even though it was soaking wet and sooty. It would need to be dried in some manner which would not cause any of the cards to stick together. If this could be dried effectively, it could be compared to the list of books salvaged to aid in making an accurate insurance claim as well as assisting in re-ordering books which had been destroyed.

Although the scene was a grim one, there did appear to be some hope of putting a library back together again. Offers had already been coming in to replace many of the volumes currently in print which covered the majority of those destroyed on the fifth floor. For this the University was grateful. The project at first looked overwhelming, however, as a result of radio and TV coverage, there were already over 200 volunteers waiting for instructions on where to begin.

The initial shock of the first inspection was over and it was time for the work to begin.

Figure 6. Damage to library on the fifth floor

CHAPTER 4

Removal of Damaged Materials

Water in spots on the fourth floor was five inches deep (fig.7) and it took a 200 person volunteer crew, two full days to box and remove all of the materials from the library. The task was further complicated by the fact that the stairs were considered to be unsafe and the elevators were inoperable. The solution was to pass the boxes of books through window openings of the fourth floor and load them into debris boxes suspended from hydraulic cranes, which had been brought in to assist in the debris removal. (fig.8,9) The debris boxes were then lowered to the ground for transfer into awaiting trucks.

Figure 7. Water on fourth floor was an inconvenience.

Since it had been determined by the Disaster Recovery Team that only a portion of the books were wet enough to be threatened by mold growth, boxes had to be appropriately marked "wet" or "dry". A short training session on what was "wet" and what was "dry" was conducted by Dr. Matthews and the work progressed.

Initially stacks were prenumbered and boxes identified to keep the books in order. This system failed early in the process for several reasons. There were not enough boxes, trained manpower, nor floor space at the emergency staging areas to unpack and arrange the library.

When the materials were received at the street level, those that had been marked "wet", were taken to Associated Freezers in Dartmouth, about 10 miles away where they were placed in cold storage at 0°F. Those that were not labeled "wet" were taken to the gymnasium on campus, unboxed, and fanned out. The Physical Education Department's equipment had been frantically removed from the gymnasium as the boxes of books were arriving. After six hours of moving books into the gymnasium, it was obvious that additional space would be needed.

Figure 8. View from above showing debris box
used for book removal

*Figure 9. View from ground showing crane and debris box
used for book removal from burned library*

By late Saturday afternoon, one day after the fire, four separate locations (approximately 20,000 square feet) on or near campus were used to store the approximately 70,000 volumes thought to be "dry"; approximately 20,000 volumes had been moved to the freezer plant. The fire damaged library was empty and volunteers gone.

The moving effort was commendable since the volunteer crew had moved over 90,000 volumes (2.5 shelf miles) within a 48 hour period after the fire. This effort enabled *all* books to be removed without mold growth.

By Sunday afternoon, two days after the fire, both time and volunteers ran out well before all of the "dry" books had been unpacked to air dry. In another of his observations Dr. Fred Matthews of Dalhousie, said:

> *"The enthusiasm of people to volunteer in a disaster seems to last for approximately 72 hours. At which time it doesn't merely decrease. It disappears!"*

On Monday, three days after the fire, about half of the dry books were still in boxes at the various locations. This was to become a real cause for concern since some of these books were discovered to be wet. By this time, there were no volunteers left.

Because some dry books were actually wet, it was important that the next step in the salvage operation was to unpack and check all books earlier thought to be dry and immediately re-sort the wet books for transfer to the freezers. This was required not only for the eventual salvage of wet books, but also to protect the dry books from contamination with mold.

It was fortunate that there were few wet books which were intermixed with those which were dry as this re-sorting project was not completed until one week after the fire. The good packing and sorting job done earlier by the volunteers had paid off well.

In retrospect the situation at Dalhousie was considerably less disastrous than that described by Waters relating to the Florence, Italy flood in 1966. There, thousands of volumes were lost to mold, mildew, and packing problems since no methods had been developed to salvage such materials properly.

The Dalhousie Disaster Recovery Team's general knowledge of how to proceed, as defined in the Waters and Barton/Wellheiser books, was a major factor in the success of the subsequent salvage effort. The tragic lessons learned at Florence were applied quickly and successfully at Dalhousie University.

Dalhousie was extremely fortunate to muster enough volunteers to complete this task without any major loss of books. The Disaster Recovery Team had very good management, but any number of uncontrollable factors might have worked against them and caused more failures than successes.

The Reasons For Dalhousie's Success During Removal Phase

1.   General knowledge of what needed to be done
2.   Immediately set up a Disaster Team to coordinate work
3.   Selected a knowledgeable person to head the Team
4.   Used trained library personnel to act as assistants
5.   Set up a command post
6.   Delegated authority/responsibility for procuring materials/services
7.   Defined each task to be done
8.   Segregated work force into task groups
9.   Had community participation
10. Used Radio/TV to call for assistance
11. Had use of heavy equipment to assist in removal effort
12. Total commitment to the removal was done quickly

CHAPTER 5

Sorting and Packing Water Damaged Library Materials

At this point a discussion of the optimum approach to packing and removal of water damaged materials is offered for those using these writings in their disaster planning effort. (Further information can be obtained in both Water's[4] and Barton/Wellheiser's[5] books.)

Box Size:

Uniform one cubic foot boxes 12x15x10 (standard record center boxes) and one and a half cubic foot boxes 12x18x12 are optimum for the overall success of a salvage effort.

1. Larger boxes (see those in the debris box in figure 8) become overly heavy and are often mishandled, particularly as fatigue sets in on the workers.

2. Wet books are very susceptible to mechanical damage! Materials that are packed more securely in a compact box have a better chance of being salvaged.

3. Boxes which are too large cause the freezing process to be slower and non-uniform.

4. Smaller boxes speed heat transfer in the vacuum or freeze drying process. Thus if packing is done in proper sized boxes, time consuming and potentially damagingrepackaging can be avoided.

5. Milk crates which are sometimes available from the dairies can be used but tend to permanently "imprint" water damaged materials with the crate design. They also do not allow even heat distribution during the drying process as do cardboard boxes.

The one cubic foot box will weigh a maximum of 50 pounds when filled with wet material. The standard record center box will accommodate either letter or legal files and most books. The maximum size recommended is 12" wide x 18" long x 12" deep or 1.5 cubic feet. Standard 200 pound test cardboard is ideal for packing boxes. (fig. 6)

When estimating the quantity of boxes needed use the following guidelines:

1. Full letter-size file drawers contain approximately 2 cubic feet, i.e. 2 boxes; full legal-size drawers contain approximately 3 cubic feet.

2. Typically 1 cubic foot will hold an average of 15 books. (If the collection is mainly law book sets or bound journals use a smaller number.)

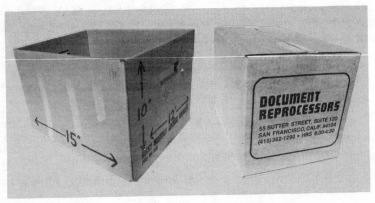

Figure 10.   Properly sized packing boxes.

Figure 11. Improperly sized packing boxes, "Too Large".

Packing:

Books should be boxed either flat or spine down to minimize damage to binding and costly repairs. Pack books of the same size next to one another to minimize warpage. Business file folders are best packed vertically. Pack boxes comfortably, never tight. Remember, swelling will continue even after the boxes are packed. Refer to the Roanoke section of this book for further information on document packing.

An illustration is provided as a guide for packing books and documents. (fig.12,13) Don't stack boxes over 4 high as they tend to collapse once the new cardboard box absorbs water from the wet contents. Shrink wrap the stacked boxes onto pallets to minimize transit damage and reduce handling costs.

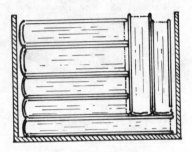

Figure 12. Proper methods for packing "wet" books.
Flat or Spine Down

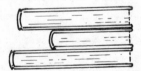 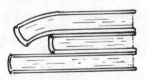

Figure 13. Improper methods for packing "wet" books.
Wet books will sag causing permanent damage

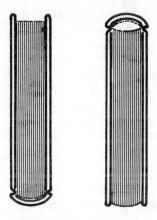

Figure 14. Spine down-good; Spine up--bad, as binding sags.

Freezer Paper:

Another procedure recommended by Waters[6] and further refined by Mrs. Sally Buchanan[7], Conservator for Stanford University during Stanford's flood in November 1978, was to interleave books with waxed paper or freezer paper. (Fig.15) The purpose is to keep book covers from freezing together and subsequently gluing together and to prevent bleeding of dyes and adhesives. (Loose parts should be wrapped with the book, or separated if it is not obvious where they belong. Also, badly distorted books can be shaped gently before packing.) Damage occurs to the covers when separation is attempted. However, most covers even though frozen together will not glue together if the books are vacuum-freeze dried.

None of the Dalhousie books were wrapped yet there were few books that actually stayed glued together after the vacuum drying had been completed. Had the Dalhousie crew spent time wrapping, probably not all of the books would have been moved from the site within the time period while the volunteer force was available. (Remember the 72 hour rule on volunteers). This additional delay may have resulted in fewer books being salvaged, and loss due to mold and mildew.

> *It is far more important to get the damaged materials well packed and into a freezer, wrapping only if time permits.*

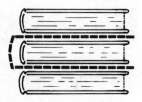

Figure 15. Proper method of wrapping books in freezer paper.

CHAPTER 6

Professional Help Arrives

After Mr. Jim Nichols, of RE-NU Associates, Digby, Nova Scotia, obtained more complete information on the fire from his contacts at Dalhousie, he again called Mr. Eric G. Lundquist of Document Reprocessors of San Francisco, specialists in the restoration of wet books and documents. (fig.16) Mr. Lundquist arrived early Monday two days following the fire and met with University officials to discuss what had been done, what needed to be done, the priorities, the time frame, and costs.

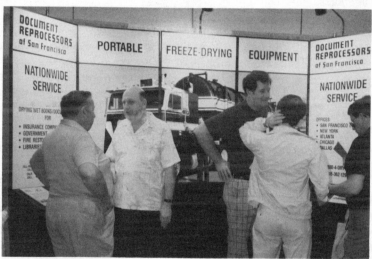

Figure 16. Jim Nichols talks with Document Reprocessors of San Francisco, during a convention in Spring of 1985.

Mr. Lundquist offered an optimistic prognosis based upon experience gained from years of experience in the salvage of water damaged books and documents, and a lifetime of dealing with disasters as an insurance adjuster. He also said all work could be done "on-site" using a unique mobile drying chamber which his firm had perfected over the last six years. As mentioned earlier, less than three days after the fire, the volunteer force had ceased to exist. The time for professional help had definitely arrived.

The following steps were taken to evaluate the Dalhousie situation:

First: Met with University officials and obtained authorization to inspect the various locations where materials had been transfered.

Second: Inspected various locations and evaluated the extent of the smoke and water damage at each site, including those in cold storage. (fig.17)

Third: Experimented with different cleaning methods for smoke and soot. Prepared samples of "before-and-after" cleaning.

Fourth: Contacted local suppliers for materials which might be needed for the project.

Fifth: Checked availability and cost of local labor from temporary help agencies.

Sixth: Prepared an action plan with timelines, mileposts, and costs.

With this information an action plan for the project was formulated. This plan would become the basis of the proposal to the University and insurance carriers. At the center of the plan were the concerns that had been expressed by University officials regarding the continuing operation of the Law School and minimizing any effects on the orderly start of the Fall term.

The plan was presented to the University. After a period of study, further questioning and reference checking, Document Reprocessors of San Francisco was selected to proceed with the project where the volunteers had left off. A tentative deadline for completion was set for October 15th; barely eight weeks after the fire. University representatives would monitor the milestones and quality control checkpoints defined in the plan.

Figure 17. Inspection of books at the cold storage plant.

Advice From The Experts

Phone calls to professional and institutional experts can save a great deal of mental anguish as well as many thousands of dollars if sought out in the earliest phases of a disaster. Do not underestimate the value of help from those who understand how to properly carry out the salvage procedures.

In the Dalhousie case, Public Archives of Canada, Ottawa, Ontario sent Mr. Geoffrey Morrow, Senior Conservator, Prints and Drawings, the day following the fire. Their support of the actions that had been initiated and advice on how to proceed was very valuable. They also participated in the final selection of Document Reprocessors of San Francisco to complete the restoration project. Mr. John Barton, Head Conservator at Archives of Ontario, visited the site later in the job.

Comments

In times of a disaster, it is important to seek and take advice of experts who have experience in handling this type of problem. Some people in higher authority have a difficult time making decisions when it comes to situations they have not encountered in the past. This is especially true in a major disaster, as quick decisions must be made, but wrong decisions are costly and will come back to haunt you.

While smaller jobs can be handled fully by an in-house staff, on the larger projects, do not fail to estimate the enormous amount of your time which needs to be devoted (almost 100% in the first phases) to getting the project defined, organized, scheduled, coordinated, supervised, and finished on time in a cost effective manner.

Also remember: Dr. Matthews 72 hour theory applies to paid staff as well as volunteers! There is nothing as old to your staff as yesterday's disaster. Most have no time, as they have already enough work to do without adding to their jobs.

CHAPTER 7

Salvage Planning

The first priority in handling this large salvage effort was to define the tasks to be accomplished, estimate how much material could be salvaged, and how it could be done. There were differing degrees and types of damage to the books. This meant that to meet the deadlines desired by the University, several different phases of the restoration effort would have to take place simultaneously.

Fortunately the 170,000 volume collection was listed on a detailed shelf list which, although water damaged, had survived the fire. In addition approximately 50% of the library holdings were computerized. Both would assist in verifying the books which had been salvaged, and help in preparation of their insurance claim.

Figure 18. Books everywhere. The task looked overwhelming.

The tasks assigned to Document Reprocessors of San Francisco were:

1. Evaluation of damage
2. Air or vacuum dry all 90,000 volumes
3. Clean all books
4. Deodorize
5. Prevent and/or eliminate mold and mildew
6. Segregate books by degree and type of damage
7. Inventory surviving books
8. Sort and box for reshelving.

The library personnel meanwhile began the task of: ordering new books to replace those on the fifth floor; ordering new shelving; seeking out new quarters as the old library was to be out of service for some months; and, starting to evaluate the problem of rebuilding the author-title and subject card catalogs.

Each phase will be discussed individually later in this book. It should be noted that these different tasks and procedures overlapped considerably and that a significant part of the project was to administer these concurrent activities effectively. The Critical Path Time Schedule (Fig.19) shows the various phases of the job, the overlapping time frame, and scheduling necessary to finish on time.

Evaluation of Damage

To prepare a complete salvage plan it was necessary to determine the extent of the damage. The following factors were evaluated:

1. Virtually all books, wet and dry, were smoke damaged to some degree. Each of the 90,000 survivors would require individual cleaning.

2. Some books in cold storage were not wet. Would it be possible to remove these from cold storage and successfully air dry them in spite of the inevitable condensation which would occur as they were warmed up to room temperature

3. 20,000 books were wet and would require drying in Document Reprocessor's large mobile vacuum drying chamber

4. 70,000 books had been exposed to excessive heat and humidity and would require air drying.

5. Conservative methods of deodorization were also considered as a cost saving method as opposed to expensive fogging with chemicals.

6. The success of mold prevention measures would also be considerably important in both the timing and cost of the project. It was hoped that the mold damage would be minimal.

7. The re-sorting and restoring to shelf order was influenced by the cleaning and drying processes. These factors were to be considered in the procedural planning.

8. Consolidation of the whole project to a single site would be desirable and needed to be considered.

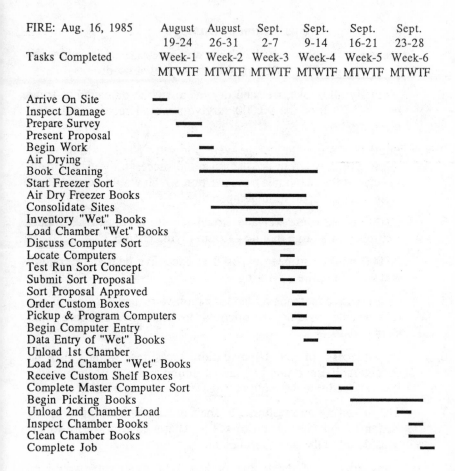

FIRE: Aug. 16, 1985	August 19-24	August 26-31	Sept. 2-7	Sept. 9-14	Sept. 16-21	Sept. 23-28
Tasks Completed	Week-1 MTWTF	Week-2 MTWTF	Week-3 MTWTF	Week-4 MTWTF	Week-5 MTWTF	Week-6 MTWTF

Arrive On Site
Inspect Damage
Prepare Survey
Present Proposal
Begin Work
Air Drying
Book Cleaning
Start Freezer Sort
Air Dry Freezer Books
Consolidate Sites
Inventory "Wet" Books
Load Chamber "Wet" Books
Discuss Computer Sort
Locate Computers
Test Run Sort Concept
Submit Sort Proposal
Sort Proposal Approved
Order Custom Boxes
Pickup & Program Computers
Begin Computer Entry
Data Entry of "Wet" Books
Unload 1st Chamber
Load 2nd Chamber "Wet" Books
Receive Custom Shelf Boxes
Complete Master Computer Sort
Begin Picking Books
Unload 2nd Chamber Load
Inspect Chamber Books
Clean Chamber Books
Complete Job

Figure 19. Critical Path time schedule for Dalhousie job.

Document Reprocessors of San Francisco • 1-800-4-DRYING

CHAPTER 8

Organizing and Training The Salvage Crews

The loss of a library or a business record center is devastating to the organizations which rely upon them. It is therefore an integral part of the salvage project that materials be restored to a useful state as soon as practical. The most successful technique for handling large projects is usually to hire locally supplied temporary help, supervised by a trained staff of professionals, who devote their entire attention to the project. This can *only* be accomplished by utilizing relatively large crews which are effectively managed.

The best approach is to start with small crews of three or four persons, and teach them the tasks to be accomplished. Once the crews have sufficient time to learn and become efficient at the operation, (usually about a day in training), the best person(s) should be selected to train new temporary personnel arriving the following day.

In full swing the Dalhousie restoration was done by 50 temporaries organized into 12 teams. The teams were supervised by a five person professional crew from Document Reprocessors of San Francisco. The end result was to dry, clean, deodorize and put 90,000 books (2 1/2 half shelf miles) *in shelf order* in just 28 working days after the fire. The drying, cleaning and deodorizing was done on site using existing techniques and the mobile drying chamber. The sorting and arranging of the books into shelf order was done by developing computer data input and sorting techniques never before used in this on such a large scale.

Each phase of the Dalhousie project was handled in this manner, with the training periods for the next phase overlapping with final completion of the prior phase, to allow for maximum manpower utilization and retention. The Salvage Crew, locally hired temporary help (fig.20) developed a school spirit which had a very positive effect on the quality as well as quantity of work accomplished. The speed at which the various phases were completed also created a favorable relationship between Document Reprocessors and the University.

Temporary Help Notes

When using temporary help it is important to remember that it is probable that none of the temporary help will have prior experience with disasters. Hence it is mandatory that proper training, supervision, and quality control checks be done on a continuing basis in order to maintain consistent quality and production.

Also remember that the temporary personnel may be young, inexperienced, sometimes immature due to their age and are not well paid. Some are employed at other jobs, or are between jobs, but if trained properly, the temporary personnel will work as an unbelievable team doing work that most ordinary staff would rebel at. Simple incentives like free coffee breaks, bonus pay, etc. are well received and minimize turnover (and associated retraining of new replacements). At Dalhousie the temporary help worked five nine hour days and received 48 hours weekly pay. Also about 15% of the crew received a cash bonus at the end of the job for staying the full duration of the job.

Temporary help was supplied by Kelly Services, who have offices world-wide. Document Reprocessors of San Francisco uses both their Light Industrial and Clerical personnel, and believes that this is the most efficient method of securing large workforces.

Figure 20. "The Disaster Recovery Team and The Salvage Crew."

CHAPTER 9

Drying Techniques: Air and Vacuum-Freeze Drying

In the Stanford University pamphlet, "Salvaging the Meyer Library"[9], Sally Buchanan writes that humidity levels in books should not exceed 12 percent at which point mold and bacteria will begin to grow. Generally, depending on location, books will have 6 to 9 percent moisture as they sit on the shelves. Tests at the unaffected libraries on the Dalhousie campus showed typical readings of 9% water in the books and 50% Relative Humidity in the air.

There are two common methods of drying books and documents: Air Drying and Vacuum-Freeze Drying.

Air Drying

The first task was to finish spreading all books to air-dry.

Air drying had already been started by the volunteers on about half or 35,000 of the books transferred to the various temporary sites on or near campus. The techniques used required standing the books up on the floor or tables with the pages allowed to fan out at a 60 degree angle.

Large commercial fans were placed in the corners of the room to create cross ventilation. The windows in these rooms were open to bring in fresh air. Daytime outside temperature was 65°F, Relative Humidity was 50%.

The effect of the fresh dry air was to equalize (reduce) the humidity in the books, even through the air was not heated. The outside air passing over the books draws the excess moisture (which had been absorbed by the book during the fire) out of the book. Heated air was not used as elevated temperatures will speed up the growth of mold and mildew in the presence of oxygen.

Figure 21. Books fanned out for air drying

The fanning of the books worked well with two exceptions. First, there was a shortage of floor space, and tables had to be set up to allow additional books to be fanned. Second, the pamphlets and soft cover books would not stand up by themselves. To solve this problem, Dr. Fred Matthews developed a wooden pegboard consisting of six inch pegs drilled into soft pine and spaced about an inch apart. Books were draped around the pegs (and in some cases the table legs), causing them to fan open, without falling over.

Overall the air drying process worked very successfully. It was a time consumming operation to fan out all the books, but was a precaution well worth it since no mold or mildew appeared. It also aided in deodorizing.

Air Drying the "Dry Books" Taken to the Freezer

A number of books taken to the freezer by the earlier crews upon closer inspection were not wet. It was later learned that the criteria for boxing was that if one of the books on the shelf was wet, the entire shelf was marked "wet". All of the books at the freezer were checked, and then books segregated into wet and dry groups. The test for wet and dry was simple. The wet books had frozen shut; the dry ones opened easily.

Sample boxes of such dry books were returned to the campus to test the success of air drying techniques, rather than dry them in the drying chamber (at a higher cost). Some of the materials from the freezer developed minor condensation because of their temperature differential relative to that of the building. The small amount of condensation did not cause any noticeable damage to the sample books and the test was considered a success. Two additional truck loads of dry books were brought from the freezer for air drying.

Notes on Air Drying

Air drying will work successfully on slightly damp or excessively humid books only. This technique is not to be used on wet books.

In the past, air drying (using plywood drying chambers or enclosed rooms) has been used for drying wet books. Using this process, warm air is passed over the books, allowing the water to migrate from the book into the drier air. This method has two major drawbacks and should only be used as the last resort on wet books.

First, the method of water transfer relies on heated air. Heat promotes mold growth, hence while the book may be drying successfully, it can also grow mold as well as transfer the mold spores from book to book. An entire collection can be contaminated if one book has an advanced stage of mold.

> *Caution:---The glues in the spine can develop mold. Since there is no way to inspect the spine without physically destroying the book, this mold may go undetected and eventually ruin the book.*

The second problem is swelling. In the air drying process, the books must be opened, either set out to fan on the floor or shelf, or strung over a nylon line (or piano wire). Drying does take place but the book swells at least 20% up to 50% and can not be successfully closed without breaking the back.

Figure 22. One of Document Reprocessors mobile drying chambers - 10,000 book capacity.

Vacuum-Freeze Drying

The mobile drying chamber used for the Dalhousie project was one of seven machines owned by Document Reprocessors of San Francisco for drying water damaged materials.

It consists of a large vacuum chamber, 45'5" long, 8'6" in diameter and 13'6' tall, mounted on a trailer chassis. The equipment is self contained having its own power source, which provides electricity to run the motors and pumps necessary to complete the process. (fig. 22 & 23) At Dalhousie, the machine was hooked up to University power.

The chamber capacity is 640 cubic feet, roughly corresponding to 10,000 books or 13 million documents. The drying cycle varies from about a week to seventeen days depending on the moisture content of the materials being dried.

In addition to three of the large chambers pictured, Document Reprocessors has just completed construction on two ocean going chambers built in the form of sea containers. These machines are also completely self contained, and do not need local electric power to operate. These are easily shipped within North America or Europe via truck, train, or ship. Their capacity is 8,000 books or 10 million documents. Two smaller chambers are also available. These will hold 500 books or 500,000 documents each and can be transported via 747 airliner.

The larger machines have completed such jobs as: Firemans Fund Insurance - San Rafael, CA.; Mission Insurance - Los Angeles, CA.; U S Naval Weapons Center - China Lake, CA.; Houston Public Library - Houston, TX.; Santa Cruz County Law Library, Santa Cruz, CA.; Washington DC Post Office; EPA - Harrisburg, PA., University of California Los Angeles (UCLA) - Los Angeles, CA.; Morton Foods - Charlottesville, VA.; Allegheny County Prothonatary (County Clerks) Office - Pittsburgh, PA.; Laramie County Clerks Office, Cheyenne, WY; New Jersey Supreme Court - Trenton, NJ; plus many other jobs, both on site or at the plants throughout the US and Canada

Approximately 350,000 books and 300,000,000 million documents have been salvaged with 98% success using this equipment since it was placed in service in 1982. Prior to that time, Document Reprocessors of San Francisco used one of its two smaller vacuum-freeze drying machines which fit into the cargo hold of a 747 airplane.

The processes used are those developed by Library of Congress, General Electric - Valley Forge, and Lockheed wherein the water in the damaged materials becomes vapor at the low chamber pressures, and is then pumped or condensed from the chamber. This allows books and documents to dry at low temperatures without damaging the materials.

Figure 23. Loading Document Reprocessors mobile drying chamber.

Humidity Checking

To check dampness, a testing gauge, loaned by Parks Canada (National Parks of Canada - Ottawa, Ontario), for measuring water content in wood, was used to estimate the moisture in the books. Moisture content was highest near the spine.

The gauge, manufactured by, Protuniter, Marlow, Bucks, and England, costs about $100.00, and is designed for checking moisture content of lumber. It is normally equipped with two sharp probes to penetrate the wood surface. "Spatula like" paddles are available for use on books but were not available for the unit loaned to Dalhousie. It was found that consistent and reliable results could be obtained by merely laying the probes gently onto the book pages which caused no damage to the books.

Rehumidifying

Books removed from the chamber after processing showed 0 percent humidity. This was expected, as the drying chamber removes all moisture in the books. There is no way to stop at the desired ambient humidity because of the varying degrees of dampness in the books when loaded into the chamber. Hence, they must be dried until all water is removed to make sure none is available to cause continued mold growth.

It is not advisable to handle the books after removal until they have rehumidified. Tests at Dalhousie, revealed that it took two weeks to rehumidify to the 9% ambient level at Dalhousie.

Dr. Robert McComb, of the Research and Testing Office of the Library of Congress, stated during a recent visit to his offices, that if faster rehumidification is needed, it can be "forced" by induction of a fine mist into the vacuum chamber during the backfilling operation as the chamber is brought to atmospheric pressure.

CHAPTER 10

Cleaning, Deodorizing and Drying Operations

The Cleaning Operation

Trials of chemical sponges were made to demonstrate to University personnel the effectiveness and safety of the technique. Results were submitted to the Disaster Recovery Team for approval before continuing. The sponges proved to be very satisfactory. Even those books with heavy smoke stain were cleaned and deemed reshelvable without further work.

Cleaning included the tops, front edge, spine, and jackets for visible smoke damage. (fig.24). There was considerable difficulty in obtaining the sponges, and several trips had to be made to the airport to pick up air shipments of the large quantities needed to complete the job.

The usual techniques for building cleanup using water washing and mild cleaners and tri- sodium phosphate (TSP) solutions do not work on books since the book covers and pages can be bleached or stained by the chemicals, especially those solutions that contain TSP.

Figure 24. A book being cleaned with a chemical sponge

Deodorizing

To reduce the very strong smoke odor which was present in the storage areas prior to cleaning of the books, it was thought to be necessary to dry fog (chemically deodorize) the rooms where the materials were stored. However, once chemical sponging on all the books had been finished, the smoke odor was virtually gone. This was welcome news to the librarians and staff, since it is generally believed that chemical processes should be considered only as a last resort for processing.

Mold and Mildew Prevention

There were many concerns about mold and mildew due to the excessive humidity in the books. Fortunately, by the time all books had been dried, cleaned, and inspected, there were less than 10 boxes of books, roughly .2% of the total which were damaged by mold and mildew. These had apparently been overlooked during the initial dry versus wet inspection. They were set aside for withdrawal, rather than risk contamination of the remaining volumes.

Salvage Results

Of the total of 90,000 books processed, only 1000 were deemed unacceptable for reshelving. The breakdown was roughly as follows:

Total Books Affected	90,000	100.0%
Books Acceptable for Immediate Reshelving	89,000	98.8%
Books Unacceptable for Immediate Reshelving	1,000	1.2%
Total Books Processed	90,000	100.0%

Of the Books Unacceptable for Immediate Reshelving:

Repairable Mechanical Damage - To Bindery	500	50.0%
Mold and Mildew - To be Withdrawn	200	20.0%
Fire Damage - Probably be discarded	300	30.0%
Total Unacceptable for Immediate Reshelving	1000	100.0%

Rare Book Collection

The above figures exclude about 3000 volumes which formed the rare book collection including first editions, and older volumes, generally those printed before 1900. Of this group, about 500 were water damaged and had been dried in the chamber. The remainder were segregated but not cleaned or inventoried. All rare books would be later inspected by a professional conservator for recommendations on future restoration of these books.

Comments:

With respect to the cleanup and drying operation, there were many major accomplishments in this phase:

First   It was accomplished by a large crew in record time.

Second   It consolidated the books into a single work area.

Third   It produced consistently acceptable quality results.

Fourth   The 98.8% success in wet book salvage may be the highest percentage ever achieved in a fire-water disaster incident.

CHAPTER 11

Mold and Mildew / Fumigation

Mold and mildew are such harmful factors in any water damaged book and document salvage project that at least a few basic facts should be constantly in mind when dealing with a disaster, large or small. Fortunately for Dalhousie, only a few books were lost to mold or mildew. (See salvage results Chapter 10 for details.)

Freezing can arrest mold development for long periods of time, but does not kill it or always prevent its advance upon thawing. Mold has been successfully thwarted by rapid freezing (before any growth has appeared) and subsequent freeze or vacuum drying (mold can not grow without oxygen which is not present in vacuum). "Blast-freezing" is most desirable if available because the smaller ice crystals yield better drying results.

Mold, a natural enemy of paper, can also spread to unaffected dry materials if neglected. *Do not underestimate the danger of mold and mildew!* Too many valuable materials have been lost by persons willing to "air-dry" or "let it dry out by itself". Once the mold is growing it is a lot harder to stop it than it is to minimize its effects by taking prompt and decisive action at the onset.

Do not succumb to the natural instinct to force hot air into areas with water damaged materials. This only spreads the mold growth.

Even if mold is not present, the conservative approach is to proceed as though it were!

The following are recommendations and observations of Mr. Peter Waters, Chief Conservation Officer at Library of Congress, and Mrs. Sally Buchanan, Conservator in charge of the Stanford University Flood in 1978.

Library of Congress Recommendations

According to Waters[8] ".. In warm, humid weather, mold growth may be expected to appear in a water-damaged area within 48 hours. In any weather, mold will appear within 48 hours in unventilated areas made warm and humid by recent fire in adjacent parts of the building.

For this reason, every effort should be made to reduce high temperatures and vent the areas as soon as the water has receded or been pumped out. Water soaked materials must be kept as cool as possible by good air circulation until they can be stabilized. To leave such materials more than 48 hours in temperatures above 70ºF and humidity above 70 percent will almost certainly result in heavy mold growth and lead to high restoration costs.

"Damaged most by these conditions are volumes printed on coated stock and such highly proteinaceous materials as leather and vellum bindings. Starch-impregnated cloths, glues, adhesives, and starch pastes are affected to a lesser degree. As long as books are tightly shelved, mold will develop only on the outer edges of the bindings. Thus no attempt should be made in these conditions to separate books and fan them open. Archival files packed closely together on the shelves in cardboard boxes or in metal file cabinets are the least affected.

"As a general rule, damp books located in warm and humid areas without ventilation will be subject to rapid mold growth. Archival files which have not been disturbed will not be attacked so quickly by mold. Very wet materials, or those still under water will not develop mold. As they begin to dry after removal from the water, both the bindings and the edges of books will be quickly attacked, by mold, especially when stored in warm, unventilated areas.

"A different problem exists for books printed on coated stock, since if they are allowed to dry in this condition, the leaves will be permanently fused together."

In situations where heavy mold is present, Waters recommends:

"Fungicidal Fogging: Where fogging is necessary, a mixture of one pound of thymol to one gallon of 1,1,1 Trichloroethane, for approximately 20,000 cubic feet, can be used. Areas to be fogged should be emptied of personnel, fans and dehumidifiers turned off, and then sealed as completely as possible. ... Six hours should elapse before the area is vented and fans and dehumidifiers turned on again. At least three more hours are necessary before salvage crews return to the building. It cannot be overemphasized that this proceedure, when necessary, should never be attempted without supervision. Appropriate safety precautions must be established and observed."

Stanford University Recommendations

Small amounts of materials can be fumigated according to Sally Buchanan, Conservator in charge of the Stanford University Flood in Nov. 1978.

"Mildew reappeared in volumes which had problems at some previous time. A 30 gallon garbage can with a lock-on lid worked quite well as a fumigation chamber. Nylon lines were strung across on two levels. The lines were placed an inch apart on each level to support books soldily, hanging open, face down. A damp towel with a handful of thymol crystals was placed on the bottom. The can held about four books at a time. They were left in five days. This method appeared to inhibit mold growth. Care had to be taken with leather bound books, as thymol sometimes softens leather unduly." [11]

Large jobs such as projects where air conditioning has been left off and mold has grown will require fogging, and possible manual cleaning and handling of each item as well as cleaning the shelving.

These problems illustrate that if mold gets started, you can be in for a major cleanup project. (fig.25,26)

Figure 25. Mold in spine of a book (not Dalhousie's).

Figure 26. Severe Mold Damage to Library Material (not Dalhousies)

Fumigation:

For many years the accepted method of sterilization was to use Ethylene oxide gas introduced into an enclosed room, trailer, etc. wherein the gas would then diffuse among the materials, killing the mold and bacteria.

The length of time of exposure varied from Corning Museums 18 hours for a total kill, to the present Library of Congress recommendations of from one to five days. After exposure the room or chambers would be ventilated, and fresh air introduced to dissipate the remaining Ethylene oxide. Thereafter, the materials could be removed and placed back in service.

In the last three years these traditional methods have come under close scrutiny with OSHA and the EPA due to recent findings involving personnel with prolonged exposure.

Present OSHA Standards Federal Register Volume 49, No. 122, Section 1910.1047, pgs 25796-25800 dated 6-22-84 limit the level of exposure to the gas to:

1:       Eight-hour TWA exposure level of 1 ppm
2:       Action level of 0.5 ppm calculated as an 8-hour TWA.

Present EPA Standards adopted in 1985 are:

1.   Flammability: above 3% concentration
2.   Toxicity: above 1 ppm in 8 hour period
3.   Emissions: greater than 1 lb. per 24 hours
4.   Disposal: hazardous waste

The effect of these recent regulations is two fold:

First, it precludes any sterilization in a confined area unless it is done in a chamber. E.g. truck and room sterilization are no longer able to meet these requirements.

Second, it now requires the operator of a sterilization chamber to comply with OSHA and EPA standards. In addition to monitoring of OSHA levels, This includes monitoring OHSA levels and will require the fitting of special apparatus at the stack discharge of the chamber vacuum pump to 'neutralize' the Ethylene oxide from entering the atmosphere. .

The methods of 'neutralization' just recently developed involve catalytic converters; chemical converters; or scrubbers. All of which are mounted on the exhaust vacuum pump exhaust. Several large companies are involved in retrofitting various sterilization facilities to meet these new requirements.

To meet these new requirements, Document Reprocessors of San Francisco has retrofitted their equipment to comply with the OSHA and EPA guidelines.

It is possible that further study by the government may eventually rule out the use of Ethylene oxide for sterilizing paper materials. However, at the time of this writing, there is no known safer and effective way of mass sterilization of flood contaminated materials except by Ethylene oxide.

Other Considerations

Mr. John Morris, author of *Managing the Library Fire Risk* notes: "The most dangerous aspect of using Ethylene oxide is its very wide explosive range, from 3% to 80% in air, so that any use of the gas in a confined space invites an explosion. A spark in a wall switch, or any other spark, would be likely to trigger a destructive explosion. Ethylene oxide is not only toxic, and a severe irritant to the respiratory tract and lungs, but it is also a source of severe dermatitis."

For alternatives to Ethylene oxide, Morris refers to a quote taken from the University of Illinois Library Services School *Friendscript*: "In a building where climate control is inadequate and mold and mildew may be present, a fungicide may be needed. Thymol has been used for this but there may be better materials. The University of Illinois had success with a product (Dowicide) suggested by the Preservation Office, Library of Congress. In crystalline powder form, 'this chemical vaporizes at room temperature, is much less expensive and less toxic than thymol, and can be quite simply deposited over a large affected area.'"

Post Fumigation Recommendations

It should be noted that materials which have been fumigated tend to outgas after removal from the chamber and should be allowed to stand in a well ventilated area for at least two days prior to return to inside storage areas.

All items which have been exposed to contamination, whether fumigated or not, are prone to a recurrence of mold and mildew growth. For this reason, care should be taken to minimize exposure to high humidity or elevated temperatures in order to preclude the growth of mold and mildew (fig. 27).

RECOMMENDATION

The enclosed reprocessed material has been subjected to flood water. Care should be taken to minimize exposure to high humidity or elevated temperatures in order to preclude the growth of mold and mildew.

DOCUMENT REPROCESSORS
ROANOKE, VIRGINIA 1985

Figure 27. Storage Recommendations for Reprocessed Material

Figure 28. "Mr. Mold"

CHAPTER 12

Putting The Library Back Into Shelf Order

In the process of removing materials from the fire, only 5,000 cardboard boxes were available, and these held only half of the collection. The only alternative at that time was to empty some of those containing dry books and to return them for refilling. This and other hasty decisions made it virtually impossible to maintain any semblance of shelf order. Hence at the onset of the project, there were 90,000 books in completely random order.

It became apparent that some method would be needed to put the library back into call number sequence. Manual reorganizing of 60,000 call numbered books and 30,000+ bound journals was decided to be impractical as there was no degree of certainty that it could be done within the given time constraints of the job (the gymnasium was needed no later than October 15th). (fig.29)

Figure 29. 60,000 cleaned books awaiting computer entry

Computers seemed ideal for this application if suitable equipment could be found and programmed in a timely and economic manner. Also, the results would have to attain a 95% confidence level, otherwise a manual system of sorting would be reverted to. (The actual level attained was 98%). The plan was to enter library "call numbers" and gymnasium location numbers into the computer database. That database would then be sorted to create a list by call number showing the location of stacks of books in the gymnasium.

This first concept of computerized sorting was an excellent idea. However, as with most ideas, it was only to become the first idea from which the final concepts would evolve. This original idea had one major drawback, it would have produced only a single list 2400 pages long. This would have been unmanageable and wouldn't have allowed the books to be put in boxes corresponding to the new shelves.

Recognizing this problem, Document Reprocessors decided that small lists, one shelf of books per page could be produced if the computer could figure out how many books to put on a shelf. Even though the computer could count, it would not have been practical to have the computer put 15, or 18 books in each box because the books varied in thickness. So each book was measured and the thickness was entered into the computer. With a little more programming, the computer was able to create its own "shelf list" by totaling up the thickness of the books once the first sort had been completed.

A dimension of 30" was used for the computerized shelf cutoff point since this dimension corresponded to 80% of a standard shelf width leaving enough room for the future expansion of a growing collection.

The thickness, stack number and call number were the three main items entered into the computer data base. Some boxes held 15 books, others 45 books. The idea worked!

By using the computer sort it was possible also to have each shelf list numbered sequentially. This would facilitate the moving of pre-numbered boxes of books into the new library with its pre-numbered shelves. In addition, many crews could fill boxes simultaneously without getting in each others way.

Equipment Selections:

The choice of which computer equipment to use was based upon several considerations not the least of which was availability:

1. *Standard microcomputers* could be used but there was the problem of carting them thorough the small aisles and the danger of power cords being disconnected causing data loss.

2. *Terminals* could be cabled directly to the University's CDC CYBER™ computer, but this was subject to delays of several days time in order to install cables.

3. *Battery powered portable lap model computers* for data entry appeared to be most likely solution. These could be "uploaded" to the CYBER™ via telephone or directly through a single dedicated line.

Once the decision to use portable computers was made, representatives of RADIO SHACK™ in Dartmouth, Nova Scotia were contacted as a source of equipment. One computer was borrowed for a test. After hearing the test was successful, RADIO SHACK™ CANADA in Barrie, Ontario generously agreed to loan the University as a public service 12 RADIO SHACK™ Model 100 portable computers (fig.30)

Figure 30. Radio Shack™ Model 100 Portable Computer

The Law Library had a computer expert, Leslie Foster, on their staff for library applications, who indicated that programming could be done in a matter of a few hours. The resulting program written in BASIC for the RADIO SHACK™ MODEL 100 computers, prompted operators line by line, with a display of the input presented before acceptance of the entry. (fig.32)

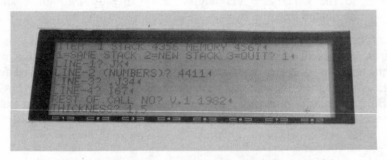

Figure 31. Operator prompts on the portable computer

A program to track input efficiency was also included as a management tool. This allowed management to check the input "efficiency" of the operators as well as the productive work time per day per operator. (fig. 33

The final programs (fig. 34,35) were tested on the Cyber at the Computer Center. It was verified that the system would work and that the sorting of 60,000 items could be done in minutes and printouts made on a high speed line printer in less than an hour.

Figure 32. Data Input Operator

Figure 33. Keeping track of data input rates

```
S H E L F

  1    390    2392  J X      4263.    .P6      W93    C.2
  2    390    2025  J X      4263.    .P7      672    C.1
  3    390    2392  J X      4263.    .P7      872    C.2
  4    390   11300  J X      4263.    .P7      C40
  5    390    9023  J X      4263.    .P7      D92
  6    390   11011  J X      4263.    .P7      D92    C.1
  7    390    9048  J X      4263.    .P7      D92    C.2
  8    390    1442  J X      4263.    .P7      F65    1970 C.2
  9    390    1442  J X      4263.    .P7      J83
 10    390    2034  J X      4263.    .P7      U32    C.1
 11    390    1442  J X      4263.    .P7      U32    C.2
 12    390    1440  J X      4263.    .P7      R45
 13    390    8065  J X      4266.    .L2      V97
 14    390    1442  J X      4270.    C73      639
 15    390    2036  J X      4270.    C73      N76
 16    390    4428  J X      4270.    .67      F84
 17    390    2034  J X      4281.    832
 18    390    2323  J X      4281.    841      C.2
 19    390    1100  J X      4281.    C85
 20    390    1106  J X      4281.    D23
 21    390    2034  J X      4281.    621
 22    390    2034  J X      4281.    G74
 23    390    1106  J X      4281.    679
 99    390   SHELF LENGTH   27.2     INCHES
```

```
 **** BOOKS SHOULD BE IN THIS ORDER IN BOX*****
TACK--IE 1440 IS AISLE 1, STACK 440
```

Figure 34. Sample of early computer generated shelf list

Document Reprocessors of San Francisco • 1-800-4-DRYING

```
              S H E L F                                      390      S H E L F
   BOOKS FROM DRYER IN THIS LIST
19  390  1106 JX   4281.   C85                          1  390  2392 JX   4263.  .P6    W95   C.2
20  390  1106 JX   4281.   D23                          2  390  2026 JX   4263.  .P7    B72   C.1
23  390  1106 JX   4281.   G79                          3  390  2392 JX   4263.  .P7    B72   C.2
12  390  1440 JX   4263.  .P7    R45                    4  390 11308 JX   4263.  .P7    C46
 8  390  1442 JX   4263.  .P7    F85   1970 C.2         5  390  9023 JX   4263.  .P7    D92
 9  390  1442 JX   4263.  .P7    J83                    6  390 11011 JX   4263.  .P7    D92   C.1
11  390  1442 JX   4263.  .P7    U32   C.2              7  390  9048 JX   4263.  .P7    D92   C.2
14  390  1442 JX   4270.   C73   G39                    8  390  1442 JX   4263.  .P7    F85   1970 C.2
 2  390  2026 JX   4263.  .P7    B72   C.1              9  390  1442 JX   4263.  .P7    J83
10  390  2034 JX   4263.  .P7    U32   C.1             10  390  2034 JX   4263.  .P7    U32   C.1
17  390  2034 JX   4281.   B32                         11  390  1442 JX   4263.  .P7    U32   C.2
21  390  2034 JX   4281.   G21                         12  390  1440 JX   4263.  .P7    R45
22  390  2034 JX   4281.   G74                         13  390  8065 JX   4268.  .L2    V97
15  390  2036 JX   4270.   C73   N76                   14  390  1442 JX   4270.   C73   G39
18  390  2323 JX   4281.   B41   C.2                   15  390  2036 JX   4270.   C73   N76
 1  390  2392 JX   4263.  .P6    W95   C.2             16  390  4428 JX   4270.  .G7    F84
 3  390  2392 JX   4263.  .P7    B72   C.2             17  390  2034 JX   4281.   B32
16  390  4428 JX   4270.  .G7    F84                   18  390  2323 JX   4281.   B41   C.2
13  390  8065 JX   4268.  .L2    V97                   19  390  1106 JX   4281.   C85
 5  390  9023 JX   4263.  .P7    D92                   20  390  1106 JX   4281.   D23
 7  390  9048 JX   4263.  .P7    D92   C.2             21  390  2034 JX   4281.   G21
99  390 SHELF LENGTH  27.2  INCHES                     22  390  2034 JX   4281.   G74
 6  390 11011 JX   4263.  .P7    D92   C.1             23  390  1106 JX   4281.   G79
 4  390 11308 JX   4263.  .P7    C46                   99  390 SHELF LENGTH  27.2  INCHES
I   S    S   <---- CALL NO ------------------->
T   H    T
E   E    A
M   L    C
    F    K

*** LIST FOR PICKING IN STACK ORDER *******             **** BOOKS SHOULD BE IN THIS ORDER IN BOX*****
STACK NUMBER OF BOOK IS A COMBINATION OF AISLE NUMBER AND STACK--IE 1440 IS AISLE 1, STACK 440
```

Figure 35. Sample of final computer generated shelf list

Operator Selection

The operators chosen for data input were a combination of typists and computer data entry specialists, all from Kelly Services temporary agency.

The actual mechanics of the data entry were to have each operator work in a separate area. The small computers were placed either on a library cart and pushed along the aisle as they progressed or held in the operators lap as they moved down the aisle, depending on operator preference. (fig.32) The operators felt it would be less confusing for them if the stacks were not prenumbered. The procedure used was for the operator to write each new stack number on a "post-it" note as a new stack was started, and to initial the note as they finished that stack. (This did prove to be a minor source of error as will be pointed out in the comments on this section.)

The computers loaned for the project were limited to about 400 entries before they had to be uploaded to the mainframe. Uploading took about 15 to 30 minutes per machine. Hence, of the 12 machines, 4 were generally "off line" being uploaded to the mainframe computer. The 12 computers provided support for a maximum of 8 operators.

There were some skeptics, as there always are, when doing something that has never been done before, i. e. the data entry process. Even with close supervision the burden of accuracy was on the operators. Speed was also very important in order to keep the salvage costs within reasonable limits. As mentioned the crew was a combination of data entry personnel and typists. Personnel trained in library science were not available. The goals were to attain an average of 4 entries per minute and an accuracy rate of over 95%. After the learning curve (about one full day) the average entry rate ended up at 3 per minute. The accuracy of over 98% was very encouraging. (This is less than the "mis-shelved" books in most libraries.) If there was any significant difference between data entry people and typists it may have been that the typists were more flexible and learned to deal with the unusual surroundings more quickly.

By the time the computerization had begun, a little over half of the books had been cleaned. The books had been placed flat in stacks on the "examination" tables with the spine facing the aisle so that the data entry crew could read the call numbers easily. Based upon the rates which had been calculated, the data entry would be completed shortly after the cleaning had been completed.

Another potential problem that surfaced during the debugging of the computer list generation process was the question of what to do about the books at the freezer plant awaiting drying. It would be necessary to include these in the sort list since they represented up to 20% of the total books to be re-organized. If they were left out, the computer generated shelf lists would be virtually useless.

The choices were either to delay data input until all books had been dried and stacked in the gymnasium or, to prepare a complete call number inventory of all frozen books which were awaiting drying. As mentioned previously, the enthusiasm to help out in a disaster becomes non-existent after 72 hours, and this applies to volunteered space as well. The library staff was already feeling a great deal of pressure to get out of the gymnasium. Inventorying at the freezer plant was the only course of action that would assure that the deadline of October 15th could be met.

Inventorying at the Freezer Plant:

Two crews of 8 each (dressed as Eskimos) were sent to the freezer plant to open boxes, unpack the books, record the call numbers in notebooks, and repack the boxes for drying.

One more problem needed to be addressed before the actual "picking" (a term used to refer to the books being pulled off the shelves or in this case tables using the computer pick list) of books could begin. In order to finish on time, the picking had to be started before all of the wet books were dried. If the computer generated shelf lists were used in sequential order, there was a good likelihood that up to 20% of the boxes would be missing books, e.g. those that were wet and were still in the chamber drying.

Since some of the books were still in the dryer while "picking" was taking place, the sorted printout was divided into two parts--one listing contained pick lists that contained at least one book in the dryer truck (about 500 shelves) and the remainder pick lists (1900) contained items solely in the gym. This was accomplished by assigning a special aisle for books in the dryer. This way all of the dry shelves were "picked" first and those from the drying chamber could be done on the last day if need be. That, in fact was the way it turned out!

As space was running out in the gymnasium it became increasingly apparent that another problem might arise if some of the books were stacked in a completely different area. It was lucky that the guess of 60,000 call numbered books was correct. Fortunately the majority of the last group of books which were cleaned ended up being journals and the final count for call numbered books was 58,300 which did just barely fit into the gymnasium. Thankfully, some of the call numbered books were inthe drying chamber.

Comments

The most significant comment about this phase of the project is that computer resorting (even if a large mainframe computer is not available) is very efficient. *It is so efficient that little or no concern should be placed on maintaining shelf order during the removal of large volumes of damaged materials.* Emphasis during the removal phase should be placed on: proper packing, speed, paper type, i.e. coated paper, and consistent determination of the "wet" and "dry" materials. The guideline being that if there is a doubt, it is "wet".

As mentioned, there were some errors in the data entry involving stack numbering. An example would be that an operator finished stack number 6199 and started the new stack as 6100 rather than 6200. A solution to this problem would be to prenumber the stacks.

Also in striving to improve upon the 98% accuracy achieved one could see that a session with the librarian regarding specifics of their particular numbering system might help to train the data entry personnel to look for certain idiosyncrasies within the system.

An example would be the case where a set of volumes exists. The call numbers will be identical except that the volume number did not appear on all the call numbers even though it is visible on the upper part of the spine. Hence, on large volume sets the computer generated shelf order would not account for individual volume numbers. Unfortunately this problem was not apparent until the picking began, which caused some minor confusion during final inspection. The impact on reshelving would be minor since the large set of volumes would be on adjacent shelves and easily rearranged manually once the books were back on the shelves.

CHAPTER 13

Picking The Books

Since trial runs had taught so much regarding data entry, it was decided to get an early start for the actual picking process. One thing needed was a trial run with the special box, 31 inches long by 8.5 inches wide and 10 inches deep, designed for the picking and short term storage of the shelves of books. It was designed with a triple wall thickness on the long sides and double wall thickness on the ends, which would insure structural stability when stacked five high (even if the bottom box was only partially full). Samples were ordered from a local box company for trial runs to test the box and picking procedures.

The first trial printouts were by call number only and tended to send the picking team on a zig zag course through the gymnasium sometimes doubling back three or four times to virtually the same location. It would be desirable and increase efficiency if the shelf list could be sorted also by stack location. To do this required a computer sort within a sort. (fig.35 see previous chapter) With a little more programming, a two sided list was produced. One side was sorted by stack number, the other side by "call number". Once the books were gathered (using the stack number sort), they could easily be put into proper shelf order (using the "call number" sort).

Two other things were experimented with during this trial run period. As mentioned the aisles were narrow in order to accommodate the very large number of volumes involved. It took a very short trial to show that the initial plan of wheeling library carts up and down the aisles would not work. If this had been done only one or two crews could have worked at a time. Shopping baskets were tried, but later the pickers hand carried the stacks of books for best efficiency.

The picking initially was done with crews of two each since many of the 5000 stacks contained up to fifteen books. This made it difficult for a single person to hold both a list and previously picked books in their arms and to still be able to pull another book without accidentally toppling the stack. Once 40% or so of the books had been picked, the pickers asked to work alone as they felt that they could produce faster that way.

The picking sequence like cleaning, sorting, computer entry, etc., was started with a small crew which was then enlarged, with the old crew teaching the new crew the techniques involved. Since the final printouts indicated 2400 shelves of books to pick, inspect, and box, production rates of 200 boxes per day were required to meet the self-imposed deadline of October 1st, giving a leeway of 15 days if something went wrong.

As with all phases of the job, the production rates were measured, and surprisingly, the "rate per man hour" with one picker was not significantly different than when there were two pickers in a crew. This did not seem possible, but additional tests verified the same result.

Once the books were pulled from the stacks, they were then set spine upward in a box lid which was custom built to fit the packing box which was 31 by 8 1/2 by 10 inches tall. This box, (fig.36) which was custom designed for the Dalhousie job held 95% of the books in their shelf order spines down. (Remember the proper packing techniques discussed earlier).

To get the other 5% packed some books had to be laid flat. This was a manual job done at the time when final inspection was completed just before stacking the boxes for transfer to the storage area. The final checking done by the Library staff included a check of book order, and a check for cleanliness (smoke removal). Only 2% of the books submitted to the checkers were returned for additional cleaning. These were then put back in line for final approval.

Final inspection and checking was done in a separate area of the gymnasium. (fig.37) The production rate was such that one checker was kept very busy checking the 200 boxes produced daily. The library actually furnished four checkers to work two hours each to cover the production time the boxing crew was working.

This system worked fine and once the books had been checked, the bottom of the box was placed into the top of the lid. The box was then inverted for shipping and storage purposes. The books then sat spine down where they could await reshelving. When the books were to be reshelved, the boxes would again be inverted, and the books would then be in proper order to reshelve without any further checking. This solution was a creative approach to the handling of the problem.

Figure 36. Custom designed shelf box

Figure 37 The Final Inspection

Comments

Although the layout used worked out quite well, some modifications would be made if the project were repeated.

First: The height of the books in the stacks should be as lowas practical within the space available. The stacks should also be of a consistent height to achieve optimum efficency in both data input and picking.

Second: A lot of space was used spreading out the small pamphlets on the tables with the books. At the end there was no room so the pamphlets were placed on edge in small boxes which in turn were given stack numbers. This later approach was much more efficient and is the way pamphlets would be handled in future projects. (Pamphlets took twice as long to handle as regular books!)

Third: The central staging area would be enlarged, as it turned out to be heavily congested. Along with this a larger final inspection station would be accommodated.

Fourth: The "post-it" notes used for numbering the stacks tended to fall off so something more reliable might be found.

Fifth: It seemed that the 8.5 inch dimension of the shelf box was a bit small (it would not accommodate loose leaf binders for example) and could be increased to 9.0 inches x 31 inches x 10 inches.

CHAPTER 14

Replacing The Shelf List and Card Catalogues

The salvaging of 90,000 books in call number order within 28 working days probably was a World Class record in library history, but there were other new concepts to come out of this major disaster. The most important concerned the rebuilding of the Library's card catalogues which had been consumed in the fire. Standard practice is to categorize their collections using three lists, commonly referred to as catalogues. These are:

> The Author-Title Card Catalogue
> The Subject Card Catalogue
> The Shelf List

The first two are usually available for public inspection as they are used to aid and assist the patron in finding a particular book, or books on the subject matter.

Information is recorded on 3 x 5 index cards with as many as eight cards per book. There are two cards for the Author-Title catalogue, several for the Subject catalogue, and one for the Shelf List. In the past these may have been made up manually by the library staff who would assign a "call number", and would decide which subject areas the books would be classified in for that particular library. (Cards were also available from library supply companies, however, the librarian would still have to assign the library's call numbers.)

All copies of a particular book in that library would have the same "call number", however the "call number" and subject classification was peculiar to that library alone, and sometimes to the classifier, thus there could be many inconsistencies within the library system. Also, the same book at another of the University's libraries, e.g. the Medical Library, might be assigned a completely different "call number" and/or subject cards.

This problem was a concern of the library system in general, and a uniform structure was developed to assure consistency between libraries. In the United States, a main step to uniformity was to assign ISBN numbers and LC numbers to each book. This facilitated determining if another library or library system had "catalogued" a particular book, and allowed libraries to purchase a standard set of cataloguing cards for their library, without having to do the cataloguing 'inhouse'.

Other improvements were to computerize library data bases and do away with the card system altogether. One highly successful conversion to computer was done by Dr. Fred Matthews of Dalhousie, about 10 years ago for the collection at Dartmouth, Nova Scotia. The visit to the Dartmouth libraries was astounding. There are no card catalogues. The Author-Title, Subject, and Shelf Lists were only available as computerized printouts updated monthly. This allowed for ease in updating the material, and removal of books that were not needed.

Dalhousies' master plan was eventually to get all books in the Law Library into the computer database, and standardized on a numbering system. The system in use was a modified LC system which the library had outgrown. Only about 50% of Dalhousie's holdings were on computer at the time of the fire. The question was whether to continue entering data, or seek another method since the other 50% still had to be done. Note: It was possible to recreate the Author-title and Subject catalogues, however this was a manual job by reading and entering all the information from the shelf list which had been salvaged. With the commercial databases available, this seemed impractical.

Dalhousie solved their problem of recreating the shelf list, as well as getting the new indexing system, by converting to UTLAS (University of Toronto Library Automated System), a computerized library system developed by the University of Toronto several years ago. Random samples of the Dalhousie shelf list were sent to UTLAS, and surprisingly, UTLAS had cataloguing information on 85% of the listings supplied. The cost was about $1.50 CND per book title.

This meant that it would be easy to develop a computerized database for Dalhousie as well as eliminate the card catalogues for the new library. The remaining 15% of the books which were not on the UTLAS system, were added to the UTLAS database using the information from the shelf list cards.

Other firms in addition to UTLAS provide automated systems, and it is believed that eventually all libraries will have automated computer generated card catalogues and shelf lists.

CHAPTER 15

What if the Disaster Is A Flood?
Roanoke, Virginia - Nov. 1985

On Nov. 4, 1985, the after effects of Hurricane Juan hit Roanoke, VA. dumping an additional 10 inches of rain after having received a record 8 inches of rain the previous three days. The swollen ground and rivers could not handle the additional water and the results were devastating.

In a short 12 hour period areas which had never flooded were under 14 feet of water, causing millions of dollars damage in a 100 square mile area. Entire towns were washed away, and the main business centers were accessible only by rowboat. Helicopters rescued numerous people from the roofs of buildings, cars were swept away, and almost three dozen people lost their lives.

Needless to say, the damage, caused by this major catastrophe, caught nearly everyone by surprise. Even if carefully prepared disaster plans were available, the results of the flood made it difficult, if not impossible, to carry them out. Most outside services e.g. trucking, boxes, refrigeration, etc. were not available. This area wide disaster experienced by the Roanoke area had wiped out much of the support needed to effect a successful salvage effort.

For these reasons, there were distinct differences between the single disaster, such as Dalhousie, and the area wide disaster at Roanoke. In Halifax there had been a community effort to get the books out of the Dalhousie Law Library. However, in Roanoke the first priority was to attend to personal losses and then worry about those of neighbors and friends.

There were things such as shelter and provisions for the homeless to be provided. Essential public services needed to be restored. The last item of priority seemed to be salvaging the books and business records, many of which were not even inspected until a week after the disaster. This was an entire community in a state of shock and bewilderment.

Like Dalhousie, materials needing immediate inspection had to wait before access could be gained to the affected buildings. Some waited for the water to recede, and others were delayed by the National Guard which had cordoned off the area as a precaution against looting. Furthermore, most of the public services were disabled: power, gas, and water had been either wiped out or turned off making initial damage surveys difficult and in some cases impossible.

Those who were prepared for a disaster, such as Atlantic Mutial Insurance Company and General Electric Credit Union, wasted no time in skipping over many preliminary steps in their disaster plans and contacted Document Reprocessors of San Francisco for assistance in the removal and eventually the drying of literally tons of water damaged documents.

A Disaster Recovery Team from Document Reprocessors of San Francisco mobilized late Nov. 4th arriving in Roanoke the following morning. Two portable Arctic 1010 drying chambers were brought to Roanoke, one from a job in Toronto, Ontario where it was finishing up an attorney's office, the second from Pittsburgh, PA., one of the Document Reprocessors' offices on the East Coast

Assessment of manpower, trucking, boxes, refrigeration services, and other temporary services were made prior to the arrival in Roanoke. The prognosis for an orderly and successful salvage effort did not look good. The flood had wiped out all local cold storage companies, most of the rental trucks in the city were under water, and many streets were still flooded and impassible. Accommodations were scarce, some of the hotels were still under water and phone service was disrupted.

It was a grim situation with widespread despair. Nothing like this had ever happened in Roanoke before.

Figure 38. Aftermath of Roanoke flood Nov. 4, 1985

It was very easy to see that this kind of disaster would present many new problems to be solved because such a wide area had been devastated. Emotions played a more significant role in the overall problem. Persons who could avoid having to work in the muddy and smelly conditions stayed away. Unfortunately many of those who were not on site were the ones with authority to decide what was to be salvaged and what was to be discarded.

Because of the magnitude of the problem, local personnel, at firms less well prepared than those previously mentioned, would not (or could not) make decisions without authorization from their Home Office. Similarly, Home Office personnel did not want to deal with the inconvenience of disrupted transportation and travel accomodations to make a site visit. Procrastination and indecision were visible were in the small as well as large firms. Not until the materials began to "smell" from mold growth did many take action. Most felt that the problem would go away by itself, as the edges of some of the materials had already air dried. It was thought that the air could dry the interior of the water damaged materials as well. It was those areas which began to grow mold and mildew.

The biggest problems to be overcome in this situation were not of a technical nature as with Dalhousie, but rather of a human nature. The problems emphasized the importance of definition of authority in any disaster planning.

Figure 39. Trucking was a problem

CHAPTER 16

Setting Up For An Area Wide Flood

The first items of business on arrival were to meet with Atlantic Insurance and General Electric Credit Union. Both had been referred to Document Reprocessors of San Francisco because of jobs done earlier in 1985 in other parts of the country.

The Atlantic Mutual Insurance Company

The Atlantic situation involved old business records in storage in one cubic foot file boxes at a local moving and storage company. Six feet of water had inundated the building damaging 8000 cubic feet of Atlantic material. Access was difficult due to lack of light and large quantities of mud in the building.

An approximate inventory was taken of the types of documents in storage and *immediate* decisions regarding the necessity of salvaging particular groups of materials were made by local and Home Office staff who had flown in to inspect the damage. Discussion later that afternoon between the local Atlantic office and their Home Offices determined what would be salvaged. These decisions were made on the basis of what was important to ongoing operations, or legally had to be salvaged. The remainder was scrapped.

Arrangements were made with a nearby box company to prepare a rush order of 2000 boxes for Atlantic's materials. These boxes sized 13"x11"x16" would handle the old, wet, file storage boxes intact. This precluded the necessity of removing, repacking, and relabeling the contents in the extremely unfavorable environment at the storage warehouse!

A crew of temporary help was hired and dispatched to the warehouse the following morning. Since the flooding had rendered the local cold storage companies inoperable, arrangements were made to rent a 45 foot refrigerated trailer for temporary storage as well as transfer of the materials to the closest available cold storage facility over 110 miles away. Three days were spent in removal of Atlantic's 1.5 million documents which otherwise would have been lost.

Refrigerated Trailers

Refrigerated Trailers: At this point, use of refrigerated trucks and trailers is discussed to alert personnel of the proper use of these, and the disastrous consequences if one relies on them for temperature reduction.

As mentioned in earlier chapters, the immediate freezing of water damaged books and documents is the MOST important step in the salvage process.

Placing wet documents into a refrigerated truck will not reduce the load temperature enough to stop mold growth. This is because the refrigeration units on the trailers are designed only to maintain the temperature of the already frozen contents. *Mold and mildew will continue to grow within the trailer.*

These refrigerator units do not have the capacity to freeze a load of wet books or documents. However, the lower temperature in the trailer will slow mold growth and is therefore an important factor in moving materials any great distance to the cold storage facility for blast freezing.

For this reason the materials must be transported quickly to the nearest cold storage facility for blast freezing. It is urgent that materials are moved to freezer facilities as rapidly as possible to limit the adverse effects of mold growth.

General Electric Credit Union

The water damage situation at General Electric Credit Union was worse than the Atlantic situaion. The area flooded was beneath the main offices and was still very slimy. Once again the lack of lighting presented a problem and the removal operations were therefore very slow. An additional inconvenience was the terrible smell encountered due to sewage contamination. All employees, Document Reprocessors of San Francisco and General Electric's, were given tetanus shots as a precautionary measure.

Decisions on what to salvage and what to dispose of were made immediately by General Electric personnel prior to the removal process. These decisions, like Atlantic's were made on the basis of what had to be legally retained. The remainder of old material was scrapped. It was evident that management was well prepared to cope with this kind of emergency. As a result, the salvage effort proceeded quite smoothly under these very adverse conditions. Two days spent at the General

Electric Credit Union offices salvaged $13 million in original loan notes which would otherwise have been lost. The Credit Union was back in operation before many businesses in the area had even fully assessed their damages.

Figure 40. General Electric Credit Union lateral files.

Figure 41. Water damaged
legal files

Figure 42. Packing damaged
materials

Figure 43. General Electric Drive Systems water damage.

The others

Other notable projects in Roanoke included the Railroad offices, a museum, banks, attorneys, oil companies, auto parts companies, General Electric Drive Systems, General Electric Service Shop, and Eli Lilly Company. Salvage crews for these jobs were supervised by Document Reprocessors of San Francisco and utilized local temporary services to pack, transport, and blast freeze the salvagable materials prior to the drying and fumigation process.

Those Who Tried Air Drying

The idea of salvaging material using vacuum-freeze drying seemed a novel concept to many. There was no doubt that it would work, but there was a reluctance to spend money for the processing of documents that appeared to have been recovered naturally by air drying. It should be noted that "formal" air drying was not attempted, what actually was tried was neglect or ignoring the problem.

The air drying approach was used by many including Eli Lilly (Elizabeth Arden Division) and by General Electric Apparatus Shop, both of whom had voluminous records to dry. Eli Lilly laid their materials out for air drying, and then repacked them. General Electric Apparatus Shop merely replaced the wet file folders with new folders.

75

Mold developed in these materials within two weeks of this attempt and required that all materials be fumigated at additional cost as well as dried. Much time and expense had been lost in trying to avoid vacuum-freeze drying, and it is fortunate that the materials were caught in time before they had been rendered useless by mold and mildew.

Others assumed materials would dry in their file drawers. Holiday Inn lost all of their materials as did Virginia Plastics and others who failed to be convinced that "air drying" would not work on contaminated materials. Bad decisions in these cases proved to be irreversible.

Temporary Headquarters - Roanoke, VA.

The large quantity of work made it feasible to bring two mobile drying chambers to the site. One was moved in from Toronto, Canada where an attorney's office records had just been dried. The other was brought from Pittsburgh, PA, the site of Document Reprocessors of San Francisco's East Coast office.

A 4000 square foot warehouse was rented for the processing, labeling, and reboxing of the materials once they had been dried. Eventually seven loads of material were to be dried. Within 12 weeks after the flood over 7 million documents were dried and returned.

Figure 44. Operations on site in Roanoke, VA.

Fumigation

The contamination of the flood waters by sewage was a major concern in this particular project. There was also some concern that mold had started in some of the materials and that fumigation would be advisable as a precautionary measure. The drying chambers, had been specially modified to meet current OSHA and EPA requirements for the handling of Ethylene oxide, which is the recommended sterilizing agent. It was recommended that materials be checked periodically for at least one year to assure that there was no recurrence of mold growth. Storage conditons of less than 70 degrees F and 50% RH must be maintained. See Fumigation Chapter 11 for further information on new regulations.

CHAPTER 17

Area Wide Disaster Versus Isolated Disaster

The important lesson to be learned from Roanoke is that in an area wide disaster, the shock of the problem has a much more serious effect on the ability to make decisions. For this reason, it is important to prepare the actions necessary in a disaster situation by developing a disaster recovery plan and referring to it once the emergency arises.

Virtually thousands of salvageable books and business records were thrown out which would eventually be necessary to reconstruct accounting records, income tax materials, etc. Others were left to air dry and then began to mold, at which point they were a total loss. Virtually all of these materials could have been salvaged if the following steps were taken immediately after the disaster occurred:

1. Obtain boxes - 1 or 1 1/2 cubic foot size preferably
2. Box materials properly identified
3. Take materials to a cold storage warehouse for freezing
4. Make arrangements for vacuum-freeze drying

Materials which are needed immediately can be dried immediately, those which can be dealt with later should be properly identified as to when they are needed.

There is no reason for materials to be discarded since the vacuum-freeze drying method can provide 98% of the materials salvaged in readable condition.

Comments

The flood or any area wide disaster, creates additional problems for any salvage crew. Also, since it usually catches people off guard, the decisions are much harder to reach than in a specific disaster situation. It is of utmost importance to have a chain of command for making decisions, whether they are right or wrong. Much material was lost in Roanoke by those who could not or would not make the decision to salvage or discard. If the decision to salvage material is not made in a very timely fashion, then the decision to discard has been made by default.

In the event of an area wide disaster even the simple problems become difficult to deal with and become complicated. Hence, if you are designing a disaster plan to cover the contingency of an area wide disaster situation be sure that it includes suppliers of goods and services who would logically be outside of the disaster area.

Figure 45. Looks ok, but lost to mold through indecision.

Figure 46. Concealed damage — eventually lost to mold.

Figure 47. Concealed damage — eventually lost to mold.

Figure 48. Left to air dry, these materials turned to mold!!

CHAPTER 18

Micrographic and Magnetic Media Recovery

The following material is used with permission from a seminar given by the Association of Records Managers and Administrators (ARMA International) in Cheyenne, Wyoming in January 1986. Subsequently it has been incorporated into the script of a 14 minute video tape entitled *"The Inside Track to Disaster Recovery"* available from ARMA. (See Appendix for addresses)

Microfilm Packout

The first step in Disaster Recovery for microfilm is to transfer the water damaged microfilm directly to plastic containers filled with clean cold water. Secure the cartons with rubber bands without removing the rolls from the cartons. This precaution prevents separation of labeling information should the cartons disintegrate.

To preserve the film for up to two weeks, add a 1 percent solution of Formalin to the water. Do not freeze the microfilm.

Microfilm Restoration

The restoration of microfilm can best be handled by a film processor capable of developing the type and size microfilm to be restored. Drain developing and fixing solutions, replacing these chemicals with clean 75 degree tap water. Remove the screeds from the processing machine to keep them from scraping off sensitive emulsions.

One roll at a time, drain the storage water from the microfilm. DON'T let the film dry out because the emulsion "fuses" to the next wrap on the roll, causing peeling of the image and the resultant loss of information.

While maintaining a constant supply of fresh water, run the film through the entire developing cycle.

Remember, the quality of these recovery films will never be as good as they were originally and will not be of archival quality. Duplication is recommended for prolonged retention.

Also note, that if film was originally purchased from Kodak, Kodak will upon request, reprocess the film at no charge according to their guarantees.

Further, due to the sensitive nature of the film emulsion, it is likely that the visual images will contain scratches and water spots, hence quality may be poor.

Microfiche and Aperture Cards

Stanford has successfully freeze dried microfiche without having to return the film through the developing process, which is difficult if not impossible. Fiche is less likely to be salvaged than film.

Much information is available from the Library of Congress on salvage of these materials which could be of help on large scale disasters.

Magnetic Media

Stabilization for *floppy diskettes* requires keeping them wet. Store floppies upright and without crowding in cool distilled water until you are ready to attempt data recovery.

As a general rule, the higher the technology, the LESS recoverable the media. Basically, the most recoverable media would be the floppy diskettes. *Discs*, or *Disc packs* might be cleaned, however the damage to the drive heads would be certain, and it is questionable as to whether one should risk trying to salvage the Disc or Disc packs because of the potential cost of replacing the heads.

The same holds true for *magnetic tape*. You may be able to wash the tape in clean water and dry it, inch by inch, but full recovery is chancy and may damage your equipment.

Basically, with magnetic media, all forms except floppy discs should be considered NON SALVAGABLE, making fixed disc or magnetic tape backup a must!

> *Never store the backups in the same general location as the originals or they may be destroyed by the same disaster. Please remember that your data discs are no good if you can't read them, hence make sure to backup your software programs as well as the data discs.*

Floppy Diskette Restoration

To restore floppies, first remove the disk from the jacket by cutting with non-magnetic scissors along the edge of the jacket. Carefully remove the diskette and agitate the exposed disks in multiple baths of cool distilled water to remove all visible dirt. Dry with lint free towels. Then insert into an empty jacket made by cannibalizing a new disc.

You need only prepare one new jacket for each five to ten discs since the same jacket can be reused several times as you copy the material from the old disc to a new disc in the computer.

Place the damaged disc in the new jacket and insert into a disc drive. Copy to a new floppy and once verifying that the information has transferred, then immediately discard the damaged disc. Label carefully. Note that you can write on the inner edge of the floppy with a permanent marker. Clean the drive heads often to minimize head damage.

Generally, most floppy diskettes can be salvaged unless the diskette itself is magnetically damaged or warped. Diskettes are made of mylar and seem to be very hearty. The Laramie County Clerks Office recently salvaged over 100 diskettes in this manner with 100% success.

CHAPTER 19

Prepare Now For Your Disaster

The old Boy Scout motto, "Be Prepared," applies very well to disasters involving books and documents. Although we would all hope never to have the occasion to use a disaster plan, the few minutes a year that need to be invested can save a significant amount of financial and emotional strain if the occasion does arise.

In order to "Be Prepared", you will need to assemble the Disaster Recovery Team and the Salvage Crew. Each person on these teams needs to know exactly what his responsibility is to be in the event of a disaster. All phone numbers, addresses, and other pertinent information on how to reach team members needs to be in the possession of each team member. Alternates need to be selected in the event that the primary member is not available. Scheduled vacation and other travel plans need to be a part of the plan. Providers of emergency supplies and services need to be a part of the plan.

We have prepared a form for your convenience which you will find at the back of this book in Appendix C. Do yourself a good deed. Photocopy the form, fill it out, and conscientiously revise it every six months (certainly not less than once a year) or when a team member has to be changed.

Pay particular attention to the sections regarding advance decisions. Some of the executives who have authority to decide what can be discarded or how much can be spent on salvage don't like to slosh around in the muddy aftermath of a flood or fire and won't be there to make the needed decisions. Get them to participate in the planning phase so that the team may proceed unimpeded.

Team members (at least the leaders) should have copies of appropriate reference materials available on their home bookshelves.

The team coordinator should have two or three names of experts or professional disaster trouble-shooters to call and discuss the extent of the loss with. At the time of the disaster, no matter how well you have prepared, you will find yourself in a state of shock. The clearer vision of a more detached expert can be very valuable to help you keep things in proper perspective.

Even if you anticipate that you will have the largest and best qualified volunteer team in history at your disposal immediately following any disaster, be prepared to be realistic that volunteers have jobs and responsibilities of their own to return to. It is also important to consider the fact that untrained or inadequately supervised personnel involved in a clean-up/transfer operation can do a considerable amount of damage (Florence Flood 1966). Paying for expert help, or at least expert supervision, could be the most important feature of your disaster plan.

When you revise your plans on a regular basis don't overlook updating your supplier list. Regulations change (some areas are starting to prohibit the storage of anything other than foodstuffs at commercial cold storage facilities). Always try to have alternate sources and plans. Make decisions about the economics of salvaging materials in a calm environment. Immediately after a disaster it is difficult to cope with concepts such as financial exposure to law suits because of missing documents.

Decisions should include:

1. Which books can be replaced more economically than they can be salvaged?

2. What are the costs (direct and hidden) of throwing something away. Remember that it costs something to sort through books and documents to determine which are of enough value to save. Costs can be as low as one or two dollars per book for drying and could easily be more than that to sort out and discard.

3. Are items available as gifts or in other formats such as microfilm.

4. What can material be tossed instead of salvaged?

5. What are the legal requirements for retention of documents?

6. Get cost estimates and set limits as a part of your original plan and then update if the disaster occurs. Considering these kinds of decisions now may even cause you to change some of your procedures for record management now so that purges can be made more rationally should a disaster strike.

If yours is a branch operation and the personnel who would make these kinds of decisions are in another city, it becomes even more imperative to get basic decisions approved and written into the plan now. Remember that mold growth can start as quickly as 48 hours after exposure of wet paper goods to air. That means 48 hours after the first fire truck rolls away or after the flood waters recede from the top file drawer.

With as little as possibly only 48 hours to pack and freeze the records and books that you are responsible for it certainly should be a high priority to get started with your disaster planning now. Disasters are definitely miserable things at the best. Don't allow one to disrupt your future any more than absolutely necessary.

Turn to the appendices now and complete your disaster planning before another day goes by.

APPENDIX A.

Summary of Emergency Procedures:

The following are items which should be considered and acted upon if required as soon as possible after a disaster strikes. These are arranged in the most logical order of priority. Common sense must be applied since each situation may be slightly different and thus could affect the order listed.

1. Contact key disaster team members.

2. Each team member contacted is to contact officals whose cooperation will be required to obtain the quickest and most accurate assessment of the extent of the damage.

3. Determine what steps need to be taken to get teams into the facility for removal of materials to an acceptable recovery area.

4. Contact the professional people whom you have designated as the consultants who will furnish you with cost estimates and information. Also determine during this step whether or not volunteers should be sought and if so for which phases of the job.

5. Set up the command center. It is preferable that this be located adjacent to the major recovery area. If it is not, the emergency phone lines should be duplicated at both locations.

6. The Disaster Recovery Team Manager and foremen start to contact sources for the materials which will be needed, i.e. boxes, plastic sheeting, workspace, hand trucks, refrigeration, trucks, cranes, etc.

7. Prepare site for recovery operations.

8. Train workers in the right methods of packing boxes for removal of materials. Include in this training any system for marking boxes relative to conditions or location of the contents.

9.   Meet to produce: a working schedule of targeted production rates, deadlines for various phases, identification of any supplies or other resources which might cause delays, assignment of team members to expedite problem items, review of communication systems available and arrangement for check-in frequencies of key personnel lacking direct communications, the issue of pagers to all who may need them, and concerns as to how the plan may fail to meet the needs of this particular disaster. Now is the time to make adjustments. Once the actual removal effort begins there will not be time to work out any details.

10.   Review any check lists which you may have. See if everything on the list is checked off that should be. Any items not yet checked off on any list should be noted and assigned deadline as well as personnel responsibility now. This information should be entered on the master schedule chart at the communications center.

11.   If there are any decisions which cannot be made by the Emergency coordinator or which need to be verified with higher managment prior to proceeding, this is the time to do it. This step could be avoided by getting approvals for salvage costs, salvage or discard, and other key decisions in the disaster plan itself. Do your best to anticipate all contingencies while working up the plan. No executive likes to make decisions under duress. A disaster represents duress of the highest order. Make the decisions in advance and delegate the authority to the emergency coordinator.

12.   Assign one person to photograph and document the process.

APPENDIX B

Suggested Disaster Recovery Team

The following should be considered a minimum of the functions to be dealt with in the formation of your disaster team. Your situation might be such that several of the functions might be assigned to one person. If that is the case be careful not to assign too much to yourself or an other single individual. There will be tasks to attend to which you can not possibly anticipate, so don't cut yourself short. Also be sure to assign alternates for all of the responsibilities.

1.   The Coordinator...The individual who is delegated the authority to make decisions on any expenditures, utilization of volunteers, hiring of any consultants, and any other financial matters. In addition this person shall be able to maintain constant communications with all other team members, and has the responsibility and authority to make decisions on what to salvage, how much money to commit to the effort, what detail is required for proper and complete insurance claims, and any other major factors involving financial impact.

2.   The Recovery Specialist...This individual should be well versed in the various types of damage which may occur in differing types of disasters. He should also be aware of the different techniques available for salvage of materials. The major responsibility shall be the recommendation of proper handling of damaged materials, the selection of any outside individuals to be used as subcontractors, approval of any deviations from the plan regarding the handling of materials, and the chief consultant to the coordinator on technical matters. Note: The coordinator may posess the same qualifications, but is involved enough in the bigger picture, particularly in the case of a major disaster, and should therefore not assume this responsibility as a dual role.

3.   The Library Specialist..The library specialist is the expert on the valuation of damaged materials which is needed by the coordinator. He also has the responsibility of conferring with the recovery specialist regarding the proper handling of particular materials. He should be the primary coordinator for the actual recovery operations, communicating all decisions and details to the secretary regarding the actual operation. He should also be the primary public relations contact in order to maintain consistency.

4.   Secretary (recorder)...This responsibility is extremely important in the proper filing of insurance claims. It is important to have one person responsible for maintaining the complete, unambiguous records of all facets of the recovery operation as well as the initial documentation and revision of the disaster plan.

5.   Operations Director...The person directly responsible for the direction of the recovery operation. Duties include supervision of volunteer work forces, employees, coordination of the activities of any others outside the institution who become involved in the recovery operation.

6.   Communications Director...Coordinates all communications. There should be a group of runners designated to act as emergency communicators, because many times the standard communications facilities will be damaged in the disaster. This person shall coordinate the operations of the runners as well as re-establishing the standard forms of communications, the procurement of temporary radio communications, installation of temporary phone and data lines etc.

7.   Institution Administration Represenative..This is the institutions represenative who will make expenditure decisions for amounts beyond those authorized for the coordinator by the plan.

8.   Institution Risk Manager...The person to whom all risk management information must be routed. This person should be actively involved in the writing of the disaster plans, risk management section, and its regular updating. He should be consulted on any matters that were not defined in the disaster plan.

9.   Building Representative...In large institutions it is necessary to have an individual on the team who has intimate familiarity with floor plans, utilities, special hazards, and any other particulars of every building managed by the institution.

APPENDIX C

The Simple Disaster Recovery Checklist

The Disaster Recovery Team and Phone Numbers:
    Leader/Coordinator: Phone Number
    Members:
                1-
                2-
                3-
                4-

The Disaster Recovery Plan

Initial Notification and Awareness

    Make Visual Damage Inspection
    Mobilize Disaster Team
    Prepare Written Damage Survey
    Prioritize Materials to be Salvaged
    Assessment of Need for Outside Help
        If yes: Make Preliminary Phone Calls — Help
        If no: Prepare for In-House Recovery

The Packout Phase

Boxing Materials - 12 x 15 x 10 inch record center size cardboard boxes, tape guns, tape, marking pens, and inventory pad. Also, label original cabinets, shelves, etc if return is to be to the same location. Substitute milk crates as an alternative to boxes. Proper packing significantly increases the recovery rate.

Support Materials: Work tables, fans, lights, dhumidifiers, handtrucks, forklift, appliance dollies, pallets, shrinkwrap (for paletizing large amounts of material).

Personnel Safety Considerations: Flashlites, rubber gloves, boots, aprons, smocks or shop coats. Maybe hard hats and masks, possibly tetanus shots.

Personnel Considerations - Other: Provide free coffee breaks; keep track of who is working as your workers like to be appreciated. Remember, the disaster adrenalin only lasts 72 hours, beyond that the enthusiasm doesn't merely decline, it disappears.

Salvage Crew: Your personnel and / or working in conjunction with Kelly Services Light Industrial Division, suppliers of temporary help.

Command Post: On Site command center for monitoring and directing the Packout effort, and answeering the hundreds of questions which seem to be asked as a result of a disaster.

Debris Removal: Shovels, debris box, dumpsters or trucks, wheel barrow, hoses, broom, squeegees, pumps.

Transportation: Trucks, refrigerated trucks or trailers to transport material to cold storage company. Note: the refrigerated units will not freeze the load, and materials must be taken to cold storage.

Cold Storage: Cold Storage Warehouse preferable with the capability of blast freezing. Look under Warehouse-Cold Storage in the Yellow Pages.

Restoration Phase:
Water Damage

Books/Documents -- Large Jobs - Locate vacuum freeze drying or vacuum drying company either to do work on site for proprietary records, or off site for non proprietary records, when time delays are not critical.

Books/Documents -- Small Jobs - Air drying and / or interleaving. Consult library or Association of Records Managers and Administrators (ARMA International) for details.

Fumigation.-- if mold and mildew growth is present. ethylene oxide is preferred but subject to stringent OSHA and EPA requirements. Fumigation is required for sewage contamination to minimize future mold and mildew growth.

Micrographic materials -- Send materials to your micrographic film processor for rinsing and drying. Kodak, Bell & Howell, or local processing lab are suggested.

Magnetic Media -- Floppy Discs only, as other forms are probably unsalvagable. Consult this book for details.

Water buckets, non magnetic scissors, dunking trays, lint free towels, new disc jackets, new discs, lables, waterproof markers and access to computer for copying the damaged disc to new discs. Discard old discs immediately after copying; clean heads often..

Fire Damage

Books and Documents: Chemical sponges for soot removal. Use paper shear, razor blades and scissors for trimming char.

Improving Aesthetics prior to return: New boxes, file folders, covers, jackets, rebinding, photocopying, etc.

Relocation Phase

Computerized reorganization and prioritization based on original inventory taken at time of Packout.

Pallets, forklift and other material handling equipment to insure fast return and minimize manpower requirements.

Return delivery schedule expectation, based on priorites, location and degree of damage, etc.

>*Note: faster action on the above means a better recovery at lower cost. Act within 48 hours to insure best results.*

Document Reprocessors of San Francisco • 1-800-4-DRYING

APPENDIX D

Sources of Assistance:

DRYING AND CLEANING:

Document Reprocessors,
41 Sutter Street, Suite 1120
San Francisco, CA 94104
Attn: Eric G. Lundquist
In California: 415-362-1290
In USA: 1-800-4-DRYING
In CANADA: 1-800-5-DRYING

Note: All restoration services from boxing and removing to reshelving/re-filing. For all types of water damage from fire to flood.

TEMPORARY HELP

Kelly Services
Light Industrial Division
Offices World-wide
Consult your local directory.

RECORDS MANAGEMENT

ARMA International
Association of Record Managers & Administrators
4200 Somerset, Suite 215
Prairie Village, Kansas
Tel: 913-341-3808
Video Film: *The Inside Track to Disaster Recovery*
$30.00, 1986

LIBRARY MATERIAL

American Library Association
50 E. Huron Street
Chicago, IL 60611
Tel: 312-944-6780

CONSERVATORS:

Peter Waters, Library of Congress
110 Independence Ave., Room LMG38
Washington, DC 22414
Tel: 202-287-5608

Robert McComb, Library of Congress
110 Independence Ave., Room LMG38
Washington, DC 22414
Tel: 202-287-5608

Don Etherington,University of Texas
Humanities Research Center,
Austin, TX 78712
Tel: 517:471-9917

Sally Buchanan,
690 Greer Road
Palo Alto, CA 94303
Tel: 415:321-2561

FOOTNOTES & BIBLIOGRAPHY

1,3,4,6,8   Peter Waters, *Proceedure for Salvage of Water-Damaged Library Materials*, 2nd Ed.,   (Washington: Library of Congress, 1979).

2,5   John P. Barton and Johanna G. Wellheiser, *An Ounce of Prevention: A Handbook on Disaster Contingency Planning for Archives, Libraries and Record Centers* (Toronto: Toronto Area Archivists Group, 1985)

7   Sally Buchanan, *The Stanford-Lockheed Meyer Library Flood Report*, (Stanford: The Stanford University Libraries, 1980)

9   John Morris, *Managing the Library Fire Risk, 2nd edition,*(Berkeley, California:University of California Office of Insurance and Risk Management,...$12.95, 1979)

Preservation Committee, New York University Libraries, *Disaster Plan Workbook,*(New York,NY: New York University, Elmer Holmes Bobst Library, Collection Management Office, 70 Washington Square South, New York, NY. 10012 $10.00, 1984)